UNDERSTANDING JEWISH MYSTICISM

THE LIBRARY OF JUDAIC LEARNING
VOLUME II

EDITED BY

JACOB NEUSNER

University Professor
Professor of Religious Studies
The Ungerleider Distinguished Scholar of Judaic Studies

BROWN UNIVERSITY

UNDERSTANDING JEWISH MYSTICISM

A Source Reader

The Merkabah Tradition
and
The Zoharic Tradition

by

DAVID R. BLUMENTHAL

The Jay and Leslie Cohen Professor of Judaic Studies
Emory University

KTAV PUBLISHING HOUSE, INC.
New York, 1978

Library of Congress Cataloging in Publication Data
Main entry under title:

Understanding Jewish mysticism.

(The Library of Judaic learning ; v. 2)
Bibliography: p.
Includes index.
1. Cabala—History. 2. Mysticism—Judaism. 3. Sefer Yezirah.
4. Hekhalot. I. Blumenthal, David R.
BM526.U5   296.1'6   78-6544
ISBN 0-87068-334-9

Manufactured in the United States of America

CONTENTS

UNIT II THE ZOHARIC TRADITION

For Ursula

Many women have done well
but you have excelled them all.
(Proverbs 31:29)

A good woman is a genuine gift.
(Talmud, Yevamot, 63b)

ACKNOWLEDGMENTS

The editor gratefully acknowledges permission to reprint excerpts from various books as follows:

"Jewish Mysticism," by G. Vajda, in *Encyclopaedia Britannica,* 15th edition, © 1974 by Encyclopaedia Britannica, Inc.;

Selections from *Zohar, The Book of Splendor,* by G. Scholem, © 1949 by Schocken Books, Inc.;

The diagram of the sefirotic tree from *Major Trends in Jewish Mysticism* by G. Scholem, © 1946, 1954; renewed 1974 by Schocken Books Inc.;

Selections from *On the Kabbalah and Its Symbolism* by G. Scholem, © 1965 by Schocken Books Inc.;

Selections from *The New English Bible,* © 1961 by the Delegates of the Oxford University Press and the Syndics of the Cambridge University Press;

Selections from *The Zohar* by H. Sperling and J. Abelson, © 1934, 1961 by Soncino Press;

The diagram of the Sunset from an anonymous, uncopyrighted pamphlet entitled *Book of Formation: The Letters of our Father Abraham;*

The diagram of the Circle from *The Book of Formation* by K. Stenring, © 1970 by Ktav Publishing House.

PREFACE

The purpose of this book is threefold: first, to present in translation some of the major texts of the Jewish mystical tradition; second, to help the concerned reader reach an understanding of these texts without having to cope with overly learned footnotes; and third, to deal with some general questions about the nature of Jewish mysticism.

To accomplish the first purpose, I have chosen appropriate texts, translating some of them from the original languages. Several of these texts appear in English here for the first time.

To accomplish the second purpose, I have written introductory and concluding notes which outline the problems of the texts and propose some answers: Who wrote this text? For whom? Why? What kind of religious experience motivated it? What is the nature of the language used? the symbolism? What is the relationship of this text to previous texts in the tradition? to other texts? What are the literary genres used in the text? And so on. To help the reader reach an understanding of these texts, I have also written an explicatory commentary to clarify the unknown terms, the strange metaphors, the elementary textual problems, as well as to sustain the conceptual continuity of the text. Depending upon the material, the commentary is either interwoven with the text or presented as notes. Throughout, I have tried to be scholarly without being inordinately technical. I have also avoided lengthy presentations of the historical, doctrinal, and literary-critical aspects of the texts because this has already been done in a definitive way by G. Scholem in *Major Trends in Jewish Mysticism*. No true understanding of the Jewish mystical tradition can be attained without careful study of the works of this scholar. And in some ways this book is intended as a reader to supplement the history of ideas presented by Scholem. Thus, Unit I draws upon chapter 2 of *Major Trends*, and Unit II draws upon chapters 5 and 6.

To accomplish the third purpose, I have asked the question: If one does not arrange the material of the Jewish mystical tradition in chronological order, how then should one arrange it? This, in turn, has led to another series of questions: What are the characteristics of this material? What sensitivities underlie it? What is "Jewish" about Jewish mysticism? What is "mystical" about Jewish mysticism? (These issues are also dealt with by Scholem in chapter 1 of *Major Trends*.) How do Jewish magic and theosophy relate to Jewish mysticism? Is Jewish mysticism necessarily personalist? What is the relationship between the mystic and the religious authorities? And so on. To insure that the answers will have some basis in the data, and to involve the reader in the exercise of scholarly judgment, I have posed these questions in the Foreword but I have answered them only in the Afterword.

The intelligent layman, the student of Judaic Studies, and the student of religion should all find interest in this book, for it provides exposure to original texts, with explicatory aids, and it deals with some of the general conceptual problems peculiar to the study of religion.

This is not a book which can be read. It must be studied, for such is the nature of the material. Mysticism is itself an elusive and complex phenomenon, and Jewish mysticism, because of its deep roots in Jewish tradition, is a very difficult area to examine. The reader must be drawn into studying, puzzling over, and then reflecting upon these texts. Otherwise, he will not understand them or the people who wrote them. If the reader is drawn into deeper study and consideration of these issues, the purposes of this book will have been accomplished.

One may well ask: Why have I gone to so much trouble to make available, at the beginning of the last quarter of the twentieth century, a group of texts which are so remote from modern man, texts whose piety and experience are probably very far from that of the reader. The answer lies in the fact that religious traditions in general, and Judaism among them, have many levels of existence. There is a certain sociological momentum to a religious tradition because people and institutions have a tendency to endure. There is also a certain intellectual momentum to a religious tradition because ideas and the intellectual molding of reality are ongoing processes. But ultimately the momentum of a religious tradition derives from the irreducibly religious experiences that it generates. Some of these experiences are more rarefied than others. Some are popular, and some are for the elite. Yet in them all, there is the contact with the numinous, the awareness of otherness, that is core and central to religious experience. As I have written (in *The Academic Study of Judaism, Second Series,* by J. Neusner, p. 88):

> Man is a being who stands not only at the nexus of nature, the intellect, and moral judgment but he is a being who stands at the nexus of the mundane and the transcendent. Man stands not only in the sunlight of this world but in the shadow of God. Man is not only the most powerful

of the animals, he is also a little lower than the angels. Humankind is the crown of Creation—the point where nature and society meet with the Force that motivates them; where mind, feeling, and judgment meet with the Presence which is their well-spring.

Or, as A. J. Heschel has so beautifully put it in *Who Is Man* (p. 66):

Existence is interspersed with suggestions of transcendence, and openness to transcendence is a constitutive element of being human.

In presenting these texts—and they represent the experience of the elite, not the masses—I hope that the reader will be able to grasp, even fleetingly, some of the grandeur, power, and indeed some of the holiness that these texts contain. The techniques and ideas may be strange to the twentieth century, but some shadow of the experience should not be too far from our awareness.

I wish to acknowledge my gratitude to the many people who have helped to make this book possible. I am grateful to my wife, Ursula, who supported me in the most discouraging moments, and who patiently typed the endless drafts of this work. To her this book is dedicated. I am particularly grateful, too, to my inquiring, open, and intelligent students. Without their searching hearts and minds, I should have become dispirited very early. I want also to express here my special thanks to my teacher and distinguished senior colleague, Jacob Neusner, who helped conceive the courses that generated this book, who saved me from many errors, and who has consistently encouraged and supported my efforts in this field. Life is a continuous learning experience, and I cannot recount or repay all I have learned from him.

FOREWORD

The study of mysticism has a certain attraction for students in the last quarter of the twentieth century. We live in an era in which we have very little control over our destinies, and the prospect of some inner domain which is truly our own is very engaging. We live in a world in which the quantity of knowledge is so great that no one can master it, and the prospect of a domain of personal consciousness which is truly ours, which is not subject to the onslaught of complex modern living, is very tantalizing. Perhaps this has always been the attraction of mysticism. Perhaps the holy man or woman, the person who has mastered the pressures of everyday life by discipline of the inner life, has always held fascination for the rest of us, who see ourselves as suffering through existence. Yet it is not so. Perhaps it was never so. Spirituality as a quality of living is won by hard work, by knowledge, by practice. Talent helps, but it is not sufficient. One must be haunted by the spiritual, fleeing it at times and greeting it joyously at others. One must be pursued by the spiritual, seeking refuge from it as did Jonah, and courageously confronting it as did Jeremiah. What is the "spiritual" which so many have sensed? What is the Reality from which so many have flown, only to be pursued?

To define the "spiritual" we must begin with language, for it is in words that we communicate. We must begin by noting that mankind communicates in many languages. I do not mean in many national tongues; I mean in many languages—in the language of art, in the language of the body, in music, in words. Yet even in the realm of words, mankind communicates in many languages—the language of beauty (aesthetics), the language of right and wrong (morality), the language of organized thought (intellect), and also the language of that which transcends human existence (the spiritual). These languages are called "universes of discourse," and each has its own vocabulary. The words of each universe of discourse appear to define each other, and they do not appear to be definable in terms of the other universes of discourse. Thus, we would not normally try to define the beautiful as right (i.e., by recourse to words from the universe of moral discourse). Nor would we try to define the intellectual by describing it as beautiful (i.e., by recourse to the universe of aesthetics). A great deal of philosophy, in its poorest sense, is devoted to an attempt to define one universe of discourse by reducing it to another. It seems, rather, that the best method of "definition" for any term is to determine the group of words into which it best fits (its universe of discourse) and then to see how it relates to other terms within that realm.

Within the universe of religious (or spiritual) discourse, we, too, have words. Ask yourself what the word *awe* means to you—being careful not to reduce it to a psychological state or a social situation. Or ask yourself what the word *spiritual* means, without reducing it to some stereotypic definition. Do the same with *wonder, mystery, faith, transcendent, blessed, joy,* etc., always being careful not to be guilty of reductionism— i.e., of reducing these words to the universes of psychology, philosophy, anthropology, or some other realm. These are the words of the universe of religious (spiritual) discourse.

The universe of spiritual discourse is also composed of images. What do the following images convey: "He leadeth me beside still water," "the great Nothingness," "Throne," "Light," "Universal Mind," "the Beloved," "Thou," "I," "Father," etc.? These are images, and they too comprise the universe of spiritual discourse.

All universes of discourse function by analogy to our own experience. We know "right" because we have experiences of right and wrong. We know "beautiful" because we have experiences of beautiful and ugly. And we know "transcendent" because we have experiences, of greater and lesser intensity, of the transcendent (and the demonic). Without experience, these terms are meaningless. With experience, they awaken an echo in another human being such that he can respond to the word or image. The other person can analogize from his own experience toward that which we are saying. All such words, then, are indicative, allusive to an experiential reality that is beyond them.

The word *mysticism* alludes to one such realm. It alludes to the realm of religious (spiritual) experience. It calls up the words and images of the transcendent, the spiritual. And it is for this reason that mysticism exercises its power. Its power derives from the experience—already had, or anticipated—in the psyche of the individual. As such, the word *mysticism* is the wrong word. We really need the word *spirituality,* or *religiosity.* This realm of discourse then is very broad, and it is *sui generis.* It is a realm of experience and of language unto itself. How shall we approach it?

We must approach the realm of the spiritual with a differentiation between the "forms of spirituality" and the "dynamics of spirituality." The "forms of spirituality" are those overt patterns of behavior which are easily identified with the institutionalized forms of religion in a society.

These patterns of behavior are no more than that: patterns, acts which the external observer can observe and record. The "dynamics of spirituality," however, are the types of mental attitude and directing of inner energies by which the individual establishes what he senses to be an awareness of, or a contact with, transcendent reality. The "dynamics of spirituality" are, in other words, the sum of attitudes and consciousness-directing techniques by which the "forms of spirituality" are transformed from overt, mechanical, social acts into acts with a transcendent dimension. These dynamics are part of the consciousness of the person performing such an act, and they are more difficult, but not impossible, for the external observer to identify. W. C. Smith has caught this distinction nicely in his differentiation between the "accumulated tradition" and the "living religious faith" within any given tradition.

The "forms of spirituality" in rabbinic tradition are many: prayer, study, *mitsva,* ethics, and so on. These "forms" can be acted out perfunctorily or they can be infused with one, or more, of the "dynamics of spirituality," and it is this infusion of mental attitude and directed inner energy which makes the act of piety full of meaning for the rabbinic Jew. It is the "Way" by which various external acts are transformed into religious experience.

Having in mind some notion of how we would go about identifying and defining the "spiritual," we can now propose the first problem which this book is designed to solve. The first problem is the identification of the terms and images of the spiritual (the transcendent) in these texts. The reader will want to ask *what* words and images allude to the realm of experience that we call "spiritual," "transcendent," "religious"? Are there differences between the *types* of spirituality represented in each of these texts? What is the underlying *dynamic* of spirituality in each case? How are they different?

The second problem is the question when does the word *mysticism* apply to this tradition? At what conceptual point, if there be any at all, can one speak of Jewish mysticism as "mystical"? Is there a difference between spiritual experience and mystical experience? Are there analogies for such a criterion from other traditions? These are very difficult questions, and not every reader will be able to answer them.

There are other questions that must also be asked, and this book is designed to provide answers to these questions too. What makes Jewish mysticism "Jewish"? What elements seem to be distinctive to that tradition? Or, to word the problematic more elegantly: What is the relationship between Rabbinic Judaism and mysticism? How did mysticism affect Rabbinic Judaism, and how did Rabbinic Judaism affect mysticism? How does each element circumscribe and set limits upon the other?

These, then, are the problems of this book: (1) to identify the terms and images in the texts which form the universe of spiritual discourse in the Jewish mystical tradition and to distinguish the types of spirituality taught; (2) to speculate upon the point at which one can legitimately use the word *mystical* in relation to these texts; and (3) to determine what is *Jewish* about these texts, to determine the way they were influenced by, and in turn influenced, Rabbinic Judaism. The reader should bear these problems in mind throughout; in the Afterword, I will attempt some answers.

Unit One

The Merkabah Tradition

GENERAL INTRODUCTION

The world of Merkabah mysticism is one of the most dazzling of the mystical worlds. It is a realm of fantastic heavenly beings, of bizarre magical names, and of occult interactions between spirit and matter. In it, closed gates to celestial palaces are opened by long, incomprehensible incantations, and the dangers which rise up against man as he enters the realm of the supernatural are met with seals of truth. It is also a world of visions—visions which are terrifying and illuminating all at once.

The selections given here are samples of two types of this literature: one deals with the secrets of Creation, and the other with the inner vision of the mystic. Throughout, there are a series of questions that the reader ought to bear in mind: First, for whom was this literature intended? And, how was it used? Second, what are its main characteristics? And what is its context? Third, what motivated it? What feelings and human insights generated this strange world? How and why did it become holy literature? And fourth, what became of this literature? What is its place in later Jewish mysticism? The General Conclusion to this unit will attempt some answers.

1

DOCTRINAL SUMMARY

Introduction

The period of Merkabah mysticism is quite extended. It may be said to begin in the century before the turn of the eras, and it continued until the tenth century of this era. Merkabah mysticism, then, covers approximately a millennium. To appreciate this fact, one may recall that all of English literature is barely a millennium old. Furthermore, the literature of Merkabah mysticism is not uniform. It includes wild apocalyptic speculation, monastic manuals, obscure numerological systems, magical incantations, as well as hymns and liturgies. Different groups, at different periods, under different influences, composed this literature. Also, many authors and editors worked on each text over several centuries.

What is this literature? Who wrote it, and where? What are its main themes? In this selection, Professor G. Vajda of the Ecole Pratique des Hautes Etudes in Paris, one of the leading authorities of this century in the field of Jewish mysticism, presents his conclusions about the literature of Merkabah mysticism. He sets forth its context and outlines its main themes. The reader will want to make note of this framework and should carefully list the technical terms used, as they are indispensable for the comprehension of this material.

The scholarly problems connected with these texts are enormous: the manuscripts do not agree, the meanings are not always known to us, and the sources—Biblical, rabbinic, and Hellenistic—for specific materials are not easily identified. The reader who wishes further information should consult: G. Scholem, *Major Trends in Jewish Mysticism,* chapter 2; idem, *Jewish Gnosticism, Merkabah Mysticism, and Talmudic Tradition* (New York: Jewish Theological Seminary, 1965); and M. Smith, "Observations on Hekhalot Rabbati," in *Biblical and Other Studies,* ed. A. Altmann (Cambridge: Harvard University Press, 1963), pp. 142–60.

Jewish Mysticism

by G. VAJDA

The centuries that followed the return from the Babylonian Exile in the 6th century B.C.E. (Before the Common Era, or B.C.) witnessed the growth and intensification of reflection on the intermediary beings between man and God, of meditation on the divine appearances whose special place of occurrence had formerly been the most sacred part of the Jerusalem Temple, of speculation on the coming into being and organization of the universe and on the creation of man. None of these themes was absent from the Bible, which was held to be divinely revealed, but each had become the object of a constant ideological readjustment that also involved the infiltration of concepts from outside and reaction against them. The speculative taste of Jewish thinkers between the 2nd century B.C.E. and the 1st century C.E. took them in many different directions: angelology (doctrine about angels) and its counterpart demonology (doctrine about devils); mythical geography and uranography, description of the heavens; speculation on the divine manifestations—which had as background the Jerusalem Temple worship and the visions of the moving "Throne" (the "Chariot," *Merkava*) in the prophecy of Ezekiel; on the double origin of man, a being formed of the earth but also the "image of God"; on the end of time; on resurrection (a concept that appeared only toward the end of the biblical period); and on rewards and punishments in the afterlife.

The literary crystallization of all this ferment was accomplished in writings, such as the book of Enoch, of which Pharisaic (rabbinical) Judaism—which became the normative Jewish tradition after the Roman conquest of Jerusalem and the destruction of the Second Temple (70 C.E.)—retained almost nothing and even the vestiges of which it tended to obliterate in its own writings; the Talmud and the Midrash (rabbinical legal and interpretative literature) touched these themes only with great reserve, often unwillingly and more often in a spirit of negative polemic.

As early as the 1st century C.E., and probably even before the national calamity of 70, there were certainly sages or teachers recognized by the religious community for whom meditation on the Scriptures—especially the creation narrative, the public revelation of the Torah on Mount Sinai,

From G. Vajda, "Jewish Mysticism," *Encyclopaedia Britannica,* 15th ed., vol. 10, pp. 184–85.

the *Merkava* vision of Ezekiel, the Song of Solomon—and reflection on the end of time, resurrection, and the afterlife were not only a matter of exegesis and of attaching new ideas to texts recognized to be of divine origin but also a matter of inner experience. It was, however, probably in other circles that speculation on the invisible world was engaged in and where the search for the means of penetrating it was carried out. It is undeniable that there exists a certain continuity between the apocalyptic visions (*i.e.,* of the cataclysmic advent of God's Kingdom) and documents of certain sects (Dead Sea Scrolls) and the writings, preserved in Hebrew, of the "explorers of the supernatural world" (*Yorde Merkava*). The latter comprise ecstatic hymns, descriptions of the "dwellings" (*hekhalot*) located between the visible world and the ever-inaccessible divinity, whose transcendence is paradoxically expressed by anthropomorphic descriptions consisting of inordinate hyperboles (*Shi'ur qoma,* "Divine Dimensions"). In addition, a few documents have been preserved that attest to the existence of methods and practices having to do with the initiation of carefully chosen persons who were made to undergo tests and ordeals in accordance with psychosomatic criteria borrowed from physiognomy (art of determining character from physical, especially facial, traits). Some theurgic efficacy was attributed to these practices, and there was some contamination from Egyptian, Hellenistic, or Mesopotamian magic. (A curious document in this respect, rich in pagan material, is the *Sefer ha-razim,* the "Treatise on Mysteries," which was discovered in 1963.) In this extrarational domain, there are many similarities between concepts reflected in unquestionably Jewish texts and the documents of contemporary non-Jewish esoterism, to the point that it becomes difficult, sometimes impossible, to distinguish the giver from the receiver. Two facts are certain however. On the one hand Gnosticism never ceases to exploit in its own way biblical themes (such as the tale of creation and speculation on angels and demons) that have passed through Judaism, whatever their original source may have been; on the other hand, though Jewish esoterism may borrow this or that motif from ancient *gnosis* or syncretism (fusion of various faiths) and may even raise to a very high rank in the hierarchy of being a supernatural entity such as the angel Metatron, also known as "little Adonai" (*i.e.,* little Lord or God), it still remains inflexibly monotheistic and rejects the Gnostic concept of a bad or simply inferior demiurge who is responsible for the creation and governing of the visible world. Finally, it is noteworthy that during the centuries that separate the Talmudic period (2nd to 5th centuries A.D.) from the full resurgence of Jewish esoterism in the middle of the 12th century, the texts that have been preserved progressively lose their density and affective authenticity and become reduced to the level of literary exercises that are more grandiloquent than substantial.

Sefer yetzira. In the ancient esoteric literature of Judaism, a special place must be given to the *Sefer yetzira* ("Book of Creation"), which deals with cosmogony and cosmology (the origin and order of the universe). Creation, it affirms with a clearly anti-Gnostic insistence, is the work of the God of Israel and took place on two different levels: the ideal, immaterial level and the concrete level. This was done according to a complex process that brings in the ten numbers (*sefirot,* singular *sefira*) of decimal notation and the 22 letters of the Hebrew alphabet. The ten numbers are not to be taken merely as arithmetical symbols: they are cosmological factors, the first of which is the spirit of God—with all the ambiguities that this term *ruah* has in Hebrew—while the nine others seem to be the archetypes of the three elements (air, water, fire) and the spatial dimensions (up, down, and the four cardinal points). After having been manipulated either in their graphic representation or in combination, the letters of the alphabet, which are considered to be adequate transcriptions of the sounds of the language, are in turn instruments of creation.

The basic idea of all this speculation is that speech (that is, language composed of words, which are in turn composed of letters/sounds) is not only a means of communication but also an operational agent destined to produce being—it has an ontological value. This value, however, does not extend to every form of language; it belongs to the Hebrew language alone.

The universe that is produced by means of the *sefirot* and the letters is constituted according to the law of correspondences between the astral world, the seasons that mark the rhythm of time, and man in his psychosomatic structure.

The "Book of Creation" certainly does not proceed entirely from biblical data and rabbinical reflection upon them; certain Greek influences are discernible, even in the vocabulary. What is important, however, is its influence on later Jewish thought, down to the present time: philosophers and esoterists have vied with one another in commentating it, pulling it in their own direction, and adjusting it to their respective ideologies. Even more important is the fact that Kabbala borrowed a great part of its terminology from it (*sefira,* among others), naturally making semantic adaptations as required.

The speculation traced above developed during the first six centuries of the Common Era, both in Palestine and in Babylonia (later called Iraq); Babylonian Judaism had its own social and ideological characteristics, which put it in opposition to Palestinian Judaism in various aspects, including esoterism as well as other manifestations of the life of the spirit. The joint doctrinal influence of the two centres was to spread during the period from the mid-8th to 11th century among the Jews established in North Africa and Europe; mystical doctrines also filtered in, but very little is known about the circumstances and means of their penetration.

2

THE SECRETS OF CREATION, PART ONE

Introduction

Jewish tradition begins "In the beginning," for in that moment, time and eternity, spirit and matter, the infinite and the finite met. What happened "In the beginning"? How did it happen? Is there some way to lift the veil and get a glimpse of the Absolute Power that brought being into being?

The author (or authors) of Sefer Yetsira did have an interpretation of the process of Creation. No one can say, of course, whether it is "correct," but the author maintains that, using his interpretation, one can oneself become a "creator," though on a much smaller scale. In other words, the Sefer Yetsira proposes not only an interpretation of "In the Beginning" but also a secret teaching of creative magic. It teaches, properly understood, the secret of Creation and of creation, of the Maker and the maker.

In order to understand this teaching, we must begin "In the Beginning," and, so, the first reading is taken from Genesis 1:1—2:5. The questions to be asked here are: What is missing from this account? Where do the angels come from? Was the water created? What else seems not to have been created? What motivated the process and moment of Creation? Why did God do it? What is the "image" of God in which man was made? And, perhaps most important: What does it mean to say "And God said"? What is speech? How did it operate? What earthly figure is the metaphoric analogy of the God of Genesis?

Genesis

In the beginning of creation, when God made heaven and earth, the earth was without form and void, with darkness over the face of the abyss, and a mighty wind that swept over the surface of the waters. God said, "Let there be light," and there was light; and God saw that the light was good, and he separated light from darkness. He called the light day, and the darkness night. So evening came, and morning came, the first day.

God said, "Let there be a vault between the waters, to separate water from water." So God made the vault, and separated the water under the vault from the water above it, and so it was; and God called the vault heaven. Evening came, and morning came, a second day.

God said, "Let the waters under heaven be gathered into one place, so that dry land may appear"; and so it was. God called the dry land earth, and the gathering of the waters he called seas; and God saw that it was good. Then God said, "Let the earth produce fresh growth, let there be on the earth plants bearing seed, fruit-trees bearing fruit each with seed according to its kind." So it was; the earth yielded fresh growth, plants bearing seed according to their kind and trees bearing fruit each with seed according to its kind; and God saw that it was good. Evening came, and morning came, a third day.

God said, "Let there be lights in the vault of heaven to separate day from night, and let them serve as signs both for festivals and for seasons and years. Let them also shine in the vault of heaven to give light on earth." So it was; God made the two great lights, the greater to govern the day and the lesser to govern the night; and with them he made the stars. God put these lights in the vault of heaven to give light on earth, to govern day and night, and to separate light from darkness; and God saw that it was good. Evening came, and morning came, a fourth day.

God said, "Let the waters teem with countless living creatures, and let birds fly above the earth across the vault of heaven." God then created the great sea-monsters and all living creatures that move and swarm in the waters, according to their kind, and every kind of bird; and God saw that it was good. So he blessed them and said, "Be fruitful and increase, fill the waters of the seas; and let the birds increase on land." Evening came, and morning came, a fifth day.

God said, "Let the earth bring forth living creatures, according to their kind: cattle, reptiles, and wild animals, all according to their kind." So it was; God made wild animals, cattle, and all reptiles, each according to its kind; and he saw that it was good. Then God said, "Let us make man in our

From *The New English Bible*, pp. 1–2.

image and likeness to rule the fish in the sea, the birds of heaven, the cattle, all wild animals on earth, and all reptiles that crawl upon the earth." So God created man in his own image; in the image of God he created him; male and female he created them. God blessed them and said to them, "Be fruitful and increase, fill the earth and subdue it, rule over the fish in the sea, the birds of heaven, and every living thing that moves upon the earth." God also said, "I give you all plants that bear seed everywhere on earth, and every tree bearing fruit which yields seed: they shall be yours for food. All green plants I give for food to the wild animals, to all the birds of heaven, and to all reptiles on earth, every living creature." So it was; and God saw all that he had made, and it was very good. Evening came, and morning came, a sixth day.

Thus heaven and earth were completed with all their mighty throng. On the sixth day God completed all the work he had been doing, and on the seventh day he ceased from all his work. God blessed the seventh day and made it holy, because on that day he ceased from all the work he had set himself to do.

This is the story of the making of heaven and earth when they were created.

Conclusion

The text of Genesis leaves many many questions unanswered: First, the waters, the darkness, the abyss, the mighty wind, and the angels, devils, and all the other heavenly "hosts" do not appear to have been created at all. Were they co-eternal with God or did He create them? If He created them, when did He do it? Second, how God created the world is not specified except by the phrase "And He said." But how did speech, which is immaterial, generate a material world? The earthly analogy of the Creator of Genesis is the fully autocratic king who commands and others obey. But was He not also an artisan, a craftsman, of His work? Third, we know nothing of God's motivation in creating the world from the Genesis story. And fourth, we have nothing but sheer speculation to use as an answer to the common element in man and God, the "image" of God in which man was made.

The Sefer Yetsira tried to answer some of these unanswered questions, and we turn to it now.

3

THE SECRETS OF CREATION, PART TWO

Introduction

The term in Rabbinic Judaism for the theme of creation is *Ma'aseh Bereshit*, which is best translated as "The Labor of Creation" or "The Mechanics of Creation." It is a term which encompasses rabbinic speculation on the mysterious beginning of all things as well as instruction for creative magic. Such speculation was kept very secret, and as a result, only hints and fragments of it have come down to us. One such fragment is presented here, the *Sefer Yetsira,* or *Book of Formation.* (For the background to Sefer Yetsira and other such fragments, see chap. 1 above, "Doctrinal Summary," and the sources cited there.) Before beginning to study this book, we must understand something of its context, its purpose, and its structure.

Sefer Yetsira has three important contexts. First, there is the Biblical context, for Sefer Yetsira was, at least in part, intended as an explication of the text of Genesis. Some of the unanswered questions of the Creation story as told in the Bible were intended to be answered by the speculations contained in the Sefer Yetsira. Second, there is the context of late antiquity, for the Sefer Yetsira is replete with concepts and ideas that are common to that milieu. Thus, numbers and letters have a central importance here, as they had in the ancient Pythagorean schools. The full extrapolation of this dimension still awaits further scholarly study. And third, both these contexts are filtered through the rabbinic world-view, that is, they are interwoven within the rabbinic view of the world as a spiritual and material order, governed by a divine Torah. Here, too, more scholarly analysis is needed for a full appreciation of this synthesis.

The purposes of the Sefer Yetsira appear to be two: the explanation of some of the aspects of the Genesis story, and instruction in creative magic.

Given these contexts and purposes, there are many questions to be asked. First, by whom and for whom was this book written? Who would write or read it, and why? Second, how does this book supplement Genesis 1? Does it make things clearer? What questions are still unanswered?

Where is God in all this? What earthly figure here is the metaphoric analogy of God? Third, I have referred to this book as a text in creative magic. How did that magic work? Why did it work? Who used it, and why? And fourth, we want to bear in mind the general questions of this whole unit: What are the characteristics of this material? What kind of impression does it leave the reader with? And what motivates this kind of text? What is its secret?

The structure of Sefer Yetsira is as follows: Chapter 1 describes the *sefirot*. Chapter 2 describes the origin and function of the twenty-two letters of the Hebrew alphabet. Chapters 3, 4, and 5 deal with the three types of letters contained in the alphabet and their respective functions in Creation. Chapter 6 is the conclusion. Each chapter is broken down into units, and each of these is called a *mishna* (pl. *mishnayot*), which simply means, "a unit of study." This is the same term used in the legal rabbinic materials.

The translation given here is my own, based upon the Hebrew texts in L . Goldschmidt, *Das Buch der Schöpfung* (Darmstadt, 1969), and *Sefer Yetsira*, anon. ed. (Jerusalem, 1964). I have also used the German translation of Goldschmidt; the English translation of K. Stenring, *The Book of Formation* (1923; reprinted., New York: Ktav, 1970); and the English translation of an anonymous, uncopyrighted pamphlet which was sent to me through the mail. The translation is accompanied by notes, which are my own, and by diagrams where I felt they would be helpful. As with many such texts, there are parts which I do not understand, and I have indicated them in the notes.

Sefer Yetsira: Text and Commentary

CHAPTER 1

1. By means of thirty-two wonderful paths of wisdom, YH, YHVH of Hosts, ELOHIM of Israel, Living ELOHIM, and Eternal King, EL SHADDAI, Merciful and Gracious, High and Uplifted, Who inhabits Eternity, exalted and holy is His Name, engraved. And He created His universe by three principles: by border and letter and number.

2. There are ten intangible sefirot and twenty-two letters as a foundation: three are Mothers, and seven double, and twelve simple.

MISHNA 1: There are three points to note here: (1) The thirty-two wonderful (or hidden) paths of wisdom are the twenty-two letters of the Hebrew alphabet plus the first ten numbers of the decimal system. (2) The multiplying of names and terms seen here is one of the characteristics of rabbinic Hebrew style. Traces of it can also be seen in the liturgy and the legal literature. Here, several names of God are enumerated. YHVH is the Tetragrammaton, i.e., the most holy and most personal name of God. It is usually rendered Yahweh or Jehovah in English. (3) The last three terms can be translated many ways. This rendering is good, but one must understand "border" to mean "boundedness." It becomes clear, then, that God created the world—i.e., made it bordered, bounded, finite—by the use of letters and numbers. Bear in mind that letters and numbers, in antiquity, are not just signs or symbols but have real existence outside our minds and, in this case, are also holy.

MISHNA 2: The Hebrew alphabet has twenty-two letters, and by the accepted rules of grammar, seven pairs of the letters have the same shape, with one member of each pair having an (extra) dot in the middle. The dot changes the pronunciation of the letter slightly (see below, chap. 4 of Sefer Yetsira). These are the "seven doubles." By the accepted rules, twelve letters have no dotted pairs. These are called "simple letters" (cf. below, chap. 5 of Sefer Yetsira). That leaves three letters which the author chose, by means not clear to us, to single out. These he calls the "Mothers" (cf. chap. 3 of Sefer Yetsira).

3. There are ten intangible sefirot: the number of the ten fingers, five opposite five, and in the center is set the covenant of the Only One with the word of the tongue, and with the convenant of nakedness.

4. There are ten intangible sefirot: ten and not nine, ten and not eleven. Understand with wisdom, and be wise with understanding, test them and explore them, know, count, and form. Understand the matter thoroughly, and set the Creator in His place. He alone is the Former and Creator. There is no other. His attributes are ten and infinite.

5. There are ten intangible sefirot whose measure is ten without end:

> depth of First, and depth of Last, depth of Good, and depth of Evil, depth of Height, and depth of Abyss, depth of East, and depth of West, depth of North, and depth of South.

Lord, Only One, EL, faithful King, rules all of them from His holy Dwelling-Place unto Eternity.

MISHNA 3: This mishna seeks to evoke some visual image although it is not clear what the image is. The "covenant of the Only One" or "covenant of the Unique One" appears to be composed of the other two elements. One element is the "word of the tongue," i.e., speech, and the other is the "covenant of nakedness," i.e., the circumcised male organ. The symbolism, then, seems twofold: (1) the covenants of the flesh and of the spirit are the main tools of creation, the one human, the other divine; and (2) the sex organ and speech are the metaphors par excellence for the creative process.

MISHNA 4: This is a magical mishna. First, the number ten is precisely set and proper wisdom evoked. Then, the reader is told "test" and "explore" (and in some manuscripts also "know, calculate, and form")—i.e., to try to combine letters and numbers and to "create" as God did. Such activity was, in fact, known in the Judaism of late antiquity. By it, some rabbis were reported to be able to create small animals and homunculi (animated clay men who cannot, however, speak). In performing these acts, the practitioner "sets the Creator in His place," i.e., becomes (in a small way) like him. The other magical mishnayot are 2:4, 5; 4:5, 10; 6:7 (i.e., chap. 2, mishna 4 and mishna 5, etc.).

MISHNA 5: Here, the basic dimensions and "borders" of reality are delineated: the physical dimension bounded by the six directions of the sphere, the temporal dimension bounded by beginning and end, and— strange though it may sound to modern ears—the moral dimension of reality, which is as basic as the physical and temporal dimensions. Note that the temporal precedes the moral, and that both precede the physical.

6. There are ten intangible sefirot whose appearance is like lightning and whose limits are infinite. His word is in them in their to-and-fro movement, and they run at His command like the whirlwind, and before His Throne they bow down.

7. There are ten intangible sefirot whose end is fixed in their beginning, as the flame is bound to the coal. Know, count, and form. For the Lord is the Only One, and the Former is One. He has no second, and before one what can you count?

8. There are ten intangiable sefirot. Shut your mouth from speaking and your heart from thinking. And if your mouth runs to speak and your heart to reflect, return to the place, for thus it is said: "And the living creatures ran and returned," and upon this word a covenant is cut.

9. There are tèn intangible sefirot. One: Spirit of living ELOHIM, blessed and blest is the Name of Him Who lives forever. (Sound, spirit, and speech, and speech is the Holy Spirit.) His beginning has no beginning, and His end has no end.

MISHNA 6: The images here are taken from Ezekiel 1.

MISHNA 7: The first image here, "end . . . fixed in their beginning," is easily decipherable: a circle, which is the perfect geometric form, is generated. The second image—the flame and the coal—is a richer image: (1) Without the coal, there is no flame (i.e., God is indispensable to the sefirot). (2) The flame is the coal in another form (i.e., the sefirot participate in the divinity of God in some way). (3) The flame fluctuates. And so on. The reader can extend his literary imagination here.

MISHNA 8: The Hebrew for "shut your mouth" is *belom pikha*, and some commentators connect *belom* with *belimah,* the term used to describe the sefirot. If this is correct, one should translate: "the ten ineffable sefirot" or "the ten self-contained sefirot." (The rendering "intangible" derives from an artificial division of the word *belimah* into *beli* and *mah*, meaning "without any thing.") Two other points are worth making here: (1) Note that it is the heart, and not the brain, which is the organ of thinking and consciousness. This is true in other rabbinic sources too, where one is told to "direct one's heart," i.e., consciousness, to God. (2) The "covenant" is the agreement of the initiates not to speak openly of the mysteries. It is an oath of secrecy.

MISHNA 9: The enumeration of the sefirot begins. Each constitutes a realm within which the Creator carries out a specific creative activity. The first four follow the text of Genesis: "And the spirit of God hovered . . ." (Gen. 1:2), "And God said," i.e., He created with words (Gen. 1:3), the "water"

10. Two: Spiritual Air from Spirit. He engraved and hewed out in it twenty-two letters as a foundation: three Mothers, and seven double, and twelve simple, and they are of One Spirit.

11. Three: Spiritual Water from Spiritual Air. He engraved and hewed out in it chaos and disorder, mud and mire. He engraved it like a kind of furrow. He raised it like a kind of wall. He surrounded it like a kind of ceiling. He poured snow over them and it became earth, as it is said, "For He said to the snow, Be earth" [Job 37:6].

12. Four: Spiritual Fire from Spiritual Water. He engraved and hewed out in it the Throne of Glory, Seraphim, and Ophanim, and Hayot, and Ministering Angels. And from the three of them He established his Dwelling-Place, as it is said: "Who makes winds His messengers, the flaming fire His ministers" [Ps. 104:4].

(Gen. 1:2, 6), and the "fire," which, according to the rabbis, was created on the second day (Gen. 1:6–8). The phrase in parenthesis is not in all manuscripts and may be out of place.

MISHNA 10: There are three terms here: "the Spirit of living Elohim" (*Ruah Elohim Hayyim*), "Spiritual Air" (*Ruah*), and "Elemental Air" (*Avir*). The first term refers to the creative spirit of God, which is, however, not identical with God Himself. The third term comes from standard ancient physics. It refers to air, one of the "Four Elements" which encircle the Earth (cf. chap. 3 of Sefer Yetsira). The middle term is complicated. It is intangible, an offspring of Spirit yet different from it, and parallel to water and fire. The function is clear; it is the realm in which the holy letters are created. Accordingly, I translate "Spiritual air" to capture its divine yet physical properties and to set it in associative sequence with the other sefirot.

MISHNA 11: Within this realm, the *tohu va-vohu* of Genesis 1:2 is created. Note that, all through this section, the Creator's activities are described as "hewing and engraving" or, better perhaps, as "hewing and stamping" (as one stamps an image on a coin). The three metaphors may refer to different visual images of the same action or to three different types of creative activity. The initiates, presumably, knew.

MISHNA 12: The Seraphim are fiery angels (Isaiah 6:2). The Hayot are the complex holy creatures, and the Ophanim are the wheels with eyes, both in Ezekiel's vision. The rabbis taught that both prophets saw all the heavenly beings. Note that God's "Dwelling-Place"—i.e., the seven palaces of the

13. He chose three of the simple letters, sealed them with Spirit and set them into His great Name, YHV, and sealed through them six extremities. Five: He sealed Height; He turned upward and sealed it with YHV. Six: He sealed Abyss; He turned downward and sealed it with YVH. Seven: He sealed East; He turned forward and sealed it with HYV. Eight: He sealed West; He turned backward and sealed it with HVY. Nine: He sealed South; He turned right and sealed it with VYH. Ten: He sealed North; He turned left and sealed it with VHY.

14. These ten intangible sefirot are One— Spirit of Living ELOHIM, Spiritual Air from Spirit, Spiritual Water from Spiritual Air, Spiritual Fire from Spiritual Water, Height, Abyss, East, West, North, and South.

---

seven heavens (cf. below, "The Chapters on Ascent")—are made from the three "spiritual elements."

MISHNA 13: Having generated the four realms (Spirit, Spiritual Air, Spiritual Water, and Spiritual Fire), and having created within these realms the letters, the primal chaotic matter of the universe, and the heavenly messengers, God now sets boundaries to space. He uses three letters of the Tetragrammaton (His Holy Name), which He infuses with Spirit. He then "seals"—sets limits—to the six dimensions of space. Note that God faces east.

CONCLUDING NOTE: What are the sefirot and what is their role in Creation? The sefirot are *not* stages in the progressive revelation of the Godhead. Rather, they are realms generated by God within which He performs His various creative acts. He acts within them as an artisan, forming and shaping His products. These realms are real, and they are, at least partially, divine. However, there are still several open questions. The text does not indicate where the sefirot come from, or how they proceed from one another. We also cannot fully resolve the conflict of imagery between mishna 5 and mishna 14.

What is the relationship of this chapter to Genesis 1? It supplies answers to the following questions: Where did the "chaos" come from? (It is not co-eternal with God. It was created out of Spiritual Water.) How did God "talk"? (He didn't. He created letters from Spiritual Air and used them, as an artisan, to build the world.) What happened before Creation? (God generated the realms, the tools, and the boundaries of Creation.) Where do angels come from? (From the Spiritual Fire.) Is this version of Creation more elegant in some way than that of Genesis 1?

Note that the initiate, too, can "create," on a smaller scale.

CHAPTER 2

1. Twenty-two letters are the foundation: three Mothers, seven double, and twelve simple.

   Three Mothers Aleph, Mem, Shin: their foundation is the scale of merit and the scale of guilt, with the tongue being that which tips the balance between them.

   Three Mothers Aleph, Mem, Shin: Mem stands still, Shin hisses, Aleph is Air which tips the balance between them.

2. Twenty-two letters are the foundation: He engraved them, He hewed them out, He combined them, He weighed them, and He set them at opposites, and He formed through them everything that is formed and everything that is destined to be formed.

3. Twenty-two letters are the foundation: He engraved them through sounds, He hewed them out in Spiritual Air, He set them through the mouth in five places:

   Aleph, Chet, Hey, and Ayin in the throat,
   Gimel, Yod, Kaf, and Kof on the palate,
   Dalet, Tet, Lamed, Nun, and Tav with the tongue,
   Zayin, Samech, Shin, Resh, and Tzade with the teeth,
   Bet, Vav, Mem, and Pey with the lips.

MISHNA 1: Neither of the images here is clear. The first seems to indicate that guilt and merit are the basic moral dimensions of the universe (see chap. 1 of Sefer Yetsira) and that it is speech (the tongue) that determines which shall prevail. The second image is even less clear. Some take it as a linguistic reference. Perhaps some breathing technique is hinted at: breathe out (Mem, and translate "is silent"), breathe in (Shin), and hold one's breath (Aleph, a glottal stop). Perhaps some incantational procedure is meant.

MISHNA 3: The sounds of these letters *are* produced at the points indicated.

21

THE WALL

ROTATION = 1   ADVANCE = 1

reverse: forward

	1	2	3	4	5	6	7	8	9	10	11	12	13	14	15	16	17	18	19	20	21
1:	8A / AB	$A / AG	RA / AD	QA / AH	PA / AV	OA / AX	SA / AT	NA / AI	MA / AK	LA / AL	KA / AM	IA / AN	TA / AS	XA / AO	ZA / AP	VA / AC	HA / AQ	DA / AR	GA / A$	BA / A&	&G / GD
2:	&B / AB	$B / BD	RB / BH	QB / BV	PB / BX	OB / BT	SB / BI	NB / BK	MB / BL	LB / BM	KB / BN	IB / BS	TB / BO	XB / BP	ZB / BC	VB / BQ	HB / BR	DB / B$	GB / B&	BG / B$	&G / OC
3:	$G / GH	RG / GV	QG / GZ	OG / GX	CG / GK	PG / GT	SG / GK	NG / GL	MG / GM	LC / GN	IC / GS	KG / GO	GT / GP	XC / GR	ZG / GC	VG / GR	HG / GS	DG / G&	CH / GR	CG / HI	RO / OQ
4:	QD / DX	CD / DT	CD / DI	OD / DK	SD / DL	PG / DM	OD / DN	LD / DS	KD / DO	ID / DP	TD / DC	XD / DQ	ZD / DR	VD / D$	HD / D&	&H / HV	DH / HT	DH / HX	CH / HI	DV / HK	RD / DZ
5:	OH / HL	SH / HM	MH / HN	MH / HS	LH / HO	KH / HP	IH / HC	TH / HQ	XH / HR	ZH / H$	VH / H&	VH / HG	RV / VT	RV / VI	CV / VK	PV / VL	PV / VM	RH / HX	CH / HT	CH / HI	PH / HK
6:	LV / VP	KV / VC	IV / VQ	TV / VR	XV / V$	ZV / V&	&Z / ZX	RZ / ZI	RZ / ZK	QZ / ZL	PZ / ZM	OZ / ZN	OZ / ZS	SZ / ZO	NZ / ZP	MZ / ZP	LZ / ZC	KZ / ZQ	IZ / ZR	TZ / Z$	XZ / Z&
7:	&X / XT	$X / XI	RX / XK	QX / XL	CX / XM	PX / XN	OX / XS	SX / XO	NX / XP	MX / XC	LX / XQ	KX / XR	IX / X$	TX / X&	&T / TI	$T / TK	RT / TL	QT / TM	CT / TN	PT / TS	OT / TO
8:	ST / TP	NT / TC	MT / TQ	LT / TR	KT / T$	IT / T&	&I / IK	$I / IL	RI / IM	QI / IN	CI / IS	PI / IO	OI / IP	SI / IC	NI / IQ	MI / IR	LI / I$	KI / I&	&K / KL	PT / TS	OT / TO
9:	QK / KS	CK / KO	PK / KP	OK / KC	SK / KQ	NK / KR	MK / K$	LK / K&	&L / LM	ML / LN	ML / LS	KZ / LR	LZ / L$	KZ / ZQ	MZ / ZP	PV / VL	PV / VM	RH / HX	CM / MN	$K / KM	RK / KN
10:	QM / MP	CM / MC	PM / MQ	OM / MR	NM / M$	NM / M&	&N / NS	$N / NO	RN / NP	ON / NC	CN / NQ	PN / NR	ON / N$	SN / N&	&S / SO	$S / SP	RS / SC	QS / SQ	CS / SR	PS / S$	OS / S&
11:	&O / OP	$O / OC	RO / OQ	QO / OR	PO / O&	OO / O&	&P / PC	$P / PQ	RP / PR	QP / P&	CP / P&	ON / NC	ON / N$	RC / C$	QC / C&	&Q / C&	$Q / QS	RQ / Q&	CS / SR	PS / S$	&& / &&

Fig. 1

4. Twenty-Two letters are the foundation:
   He set them in a wheel, like a kind of wall, with two hundred and
   thirty-one gates. And the wheel rotates forward and backward. And
   the sign of the thing is:
   —there is no goodness above pleasure ('NG) and
   —there is no evil below pain (NG').

5. How did He combine them, weigh them and set them at opposites?
   Aleph with all of them, and all of them with Aleph,
   Bet with all of them, and all of them with Bet.
   It rotates in turn, and thus they are in two hundred and thirty-one gates.
   And everything that is formed and everything that is spoken goes out
   from one term.

MISHNAYOT 4 and 5: The "gates" described here are the gates to creative activity, and the assumption is that, if one can combine the letters properly, one can reenact the creative process used by God Himself in the formation of the world. To understand this text, one must distinguish between the "basic arrangement" of the letters in "combinations" and "gates," and the "basic forms" by which the arrangement is presented, the "wall" and the "wheel."

The "combinations" are formed by combining each letter with all the other letters in the alphabet. This yields 462 "combinations" (22 letters × 21 other letters). By eliminating all the mirror images (e.g., AB, BA), one arrives at the required 231 "combinations." Alternately, one can combine each letter of the alphabet only with all those letters which follow it. Using the English alphabet, this generates the series: AB, AC, AD, . . . BC, BD, BE, . . . XY, XZ . . . YZ. This is the meaning of the text "Aleph with all of them, Bet with all of them," etc. However, the text also says, "All of them with Aleph, all of them with Bet," etc. So one must construct another set of "combinations," using the same principle but beginning at the end of the alphabet. Again using the English alphabet, this generates the series: ZY, ZX, ZW . . . YX, YW, YV . . . CB, CA . . . BA. This pairing of letters, forward and reverse, then, generates the "combinations."

The "gates" are formed by pairing the pairs of the forward and reverse "combinations." This is illustrated in Figure 1, where the upper line represents the reverse "combinations," and the lower line represents the forward "combinations." So much for the "basic arrangement" of the letters.

As to the "basic forms," the word "wall" suggests a chart, and Figure 1 illustrates that. The word "wheel" suggests a spokelike arrangement, and Figures 2 and 3 show the forward and reverse combinations displayed in

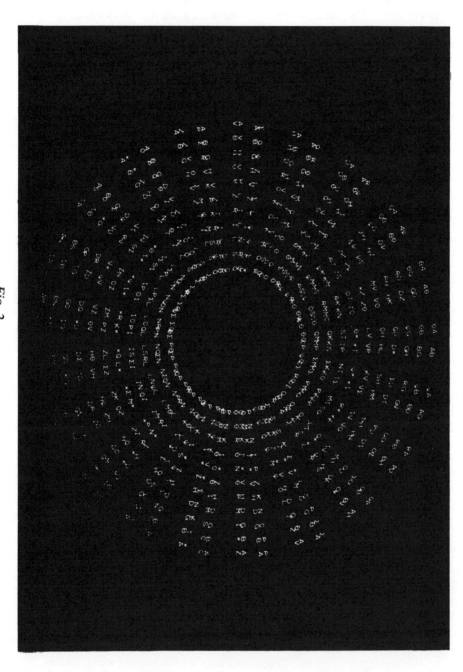

Fig. 2

THE WHEEL (BIRD'S-EYE VIEW)

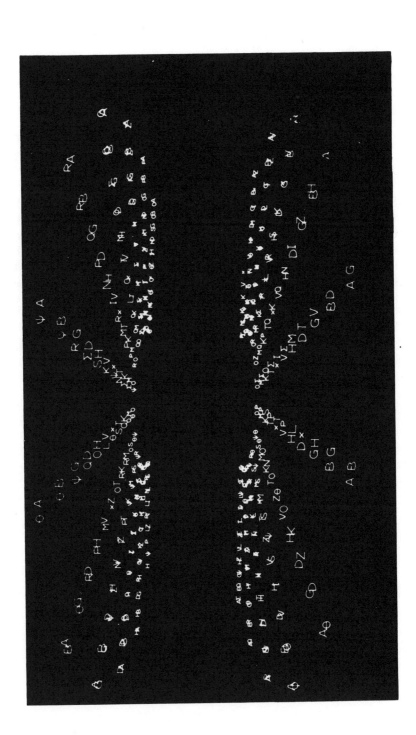

THE WHEEL (EYE-LEVEL VIEW)

Fig. 3

6. He formed substance from chaos and made that which is not into that which is. And He hewed out great columns from Air which is not tangible. And this is the sign:.

    He looks and speaks, and He makes everything that is formed and everything that is spoken with One term. And the sign of the thing is twenty-two needs in one body.

---

that form. My thanks to Harry Sparks and Russ Burns of the Brown University computer labs for their help.

But what is the key? Which is the magical chart (or magical position of the wheels)? The text hints that when 'NG and NG' have been brought into some kind of balance, the "proper" position has been found. By shifting the "combinations" of the "gates" eighteen times to the right, one arrives at the "proper" point, i.e., the point where 'NG and NG' appear. This is illustrated in Figures 4, 5, 6 at the arrows. Again, my thanks to Harry Sparks, who designed the program that provided the solution to this ancient puzzle. (N.B. The transliteration of the Hebrew characters varies from figure to figure because of the limits of the computer.)

The "one term" referred to here is probably the alphabet.

For another interpretation of this magic circle, see Figure 7, taken from Stenring's translation. I do not know how to read this diagram accurately despite Stenring's explanations.

MISHNA 6: Here, God begins to make concrete things from chaos. The first thing He makes is columns to support the physical universe. These He makes from "elemental air," here called "Air which is not tangible" to differentiate it from "atmospheric air." The twenty-two needs of the body are not specified, although whatever they are, they correspond to the twenty-two letters of the alphabet.

THE MAGIC WALL

ROTATION = 18   ADVANCE = 1

reverse: forward

	1	2	3	4	5	6	7	8	9	10	11	12	13	14	15	16	17	18	19	20	21
1:	HA/AB	DA/AG	GA/AD	BA/AH	&A/AV	$A/AZ	RA/AX	QA/AT	CA/AI	PA/AK	OA/AL	SA/AM	NA/AN	MA/AS	LA/AO	KA/AP	IA/AC	TA/AQ	XA/AR	ZA/A$	VA/A&
2:	HB/BG	DB/BD	GB/BH	&G/BV	&B/BZ	$B/BX	RB/BT	QB/BI	CB/BK	PB/BL	OB/BM	SB/BN	NB/BS	MB/BO	·LB/BP	KB/BC	IB/BQ	TB/BR	XB/B$	ZB/B&	VB/GD
3:	DG/GH	&D/GV	$D/GZ	RD/GX	$G/GT	RG/GI	QG/GK	CG/GL	PG/GM	OG/GN	SG/GS	NG/GO	MG/GP	LG/GC	KG/GQ	IG/GR	TG/G$	XG/G&	ZG/DH	VG/DV	HG/DZ
4:	RH/DX	QH/DT	CH/DI	PH/DK	QD/DL	CD/DM	PD/DN	OD/DS	SD/DO	ND/DP	MD/DC	LD/DQ	KD/DR	ID/D$	TD/D&	XD/HV	ZD/HZ	VD/HX	HD/HT	&H/HI	$H/HK
5:	OV/HL	SV/HM	NV/HN	MV/HS	OH/HO	SH/HP	NH/HC	MH/HQ	LH/HR	KH/H$	IH/H&	TH/VZ	XH/VX	ZH/VT	VH/VI	&V/VK	$V/VL	RV/VM	QV/VN	CV/VS	PV/VO
6:	KZ/VP	IZ/VC	TZ/VQ	XZ/VR	LV/V$	KV/V&	IV/ZX	TV/ZT	XV/ZI	ZV/ZK	&Z/ZL	$Z/ZM	RZ/ZN	QZ/ZS	CZ/ZO	PZ/ZP	OZ/ZC	SZ/ZQ	NZ/ZR	MZ/Z$	LZ/Z&
7:	QT/XT	CT/XI	PT/XK	OT/XL	&X/XM	$X/XN	RX/XS	QX/XO	CX/XP	PX/XC	OX/XQ	SX/XR	NX/X$	MX/X&	LX/TI	KX/TK	IX/TL	TX/TM	&T/TN	$T/TS	RT/TO
8:	KI/TP	&K/TC	$K/TQ	RK/TR	ST/TS	NT/T&	MT/IK	LT/IL	KT/IM	IT/IN	&I/IS	$I/IO	RI/IP	QI/IC	CI/IQ	PI/IR	OI/I$	SI/I&	NI/KL	MI/KM	LI/KN
9:	ML/KS	&M/KO	$M/KP	RM/KC	QK/KQ	CK/KR	PK/K$	OK/K&	SK/LM	NK/LN	MK/LS	LK/LO	&L/LP	$L/LC	RL/LQ	QL/LR	CL/L$	PL/L&	OL/MN	SL/MS	NL/MO
10:	QS/MP	CS/MC	PS/MQ	OS/MR	QM/M$	CM/M&	PM/NS	OM/NO	SM/NP	NM/NC	&N/NQ	$N/NR	RN/NS	QN/N&	CN/SO	PN/SP	ON/SC	SN/SQ	&S/SR	$S/$$	RS/S&
11:	RQ/OP	&R/OC	$R/OQ	&$/OR	&O/OS	$O/O&	RO/PC	QO/PQ	CO/PR	PO/P$	&P/P&	$P/CQ	RP/CR	QP/C$	CP/C&	&C/QR	$C/QS	RC/Q&	QC/R$	&Q/R&	$Q/$&

Fig. 4

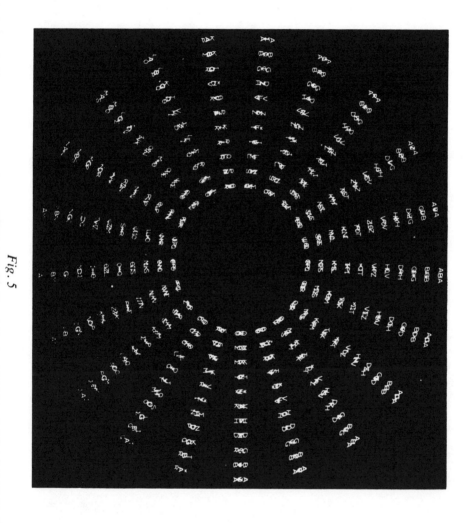

Fig. 5

THE MAGIC WHEEL (BIRD'S-EYE VIEW)

THE MAGIC WHEEL (EYE-LEVEL VIEW)

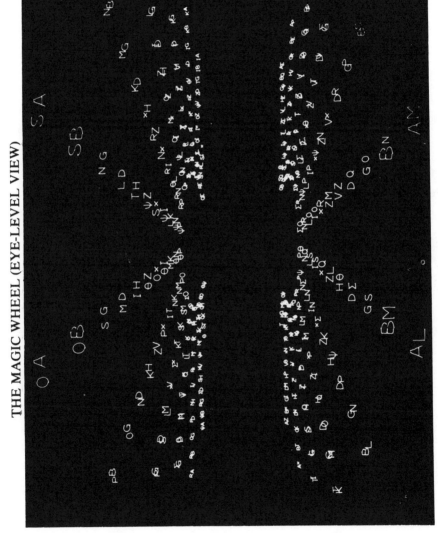

Fig. 6

THE WHEEL (ANOTHER VERSION)

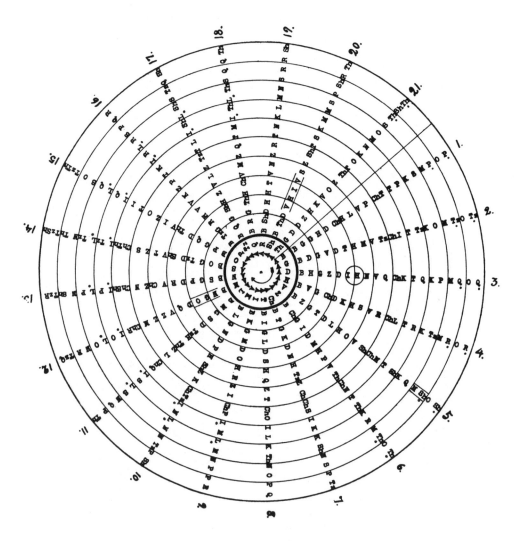

Fig. 7

From K. Stenring, *The Book of Formation* (1923; reprint, New York: Ktav, 1970) p. 21.

CHAPTER 3

1. Three Mothers: Aleph, Mem, Shin—their foundation is the scale of merit and the scale of guilt, with the tongue being that which tips the balance between them.

2. Three Mothers: Aleph, Mem, Shin—a great secret, wonderful and concealed, and He seals with six rings. And from them go out, Air, Fire, and Water. From them the Fathers are born, and from the Fathers, the Progeny. Know, count, and form, for the fire bears the water.

MISHNA 2: The "six rings" are the six directions or borders, or the six combinations of YHV.

The sequence in this chapter is as follows: The three Mothers rule over three Elements. From them, basic physical reality (the Fathers) is generated in three dimensions: in the physical universe, in the year (i.e., the seasons), and in the body. From the Fathers, flows the rest of physical reality. The following chart illustrates this (see Stenring, *The Book of Formation,* for similar charts):

Mothers	Aleph	Mem	Shin
Elements			
Fathers in the universe in the year in the body			

The author presents this sequence from two points of view—in mishnayot 5—7 from the point of view of the balanced triad, and in mishnayot 8—10 from the point of view of the creative process.

3. Three Mothers: Aleph, Mem, Shin: He engraved them, He hewed them out, He combined them, He weighed them, and He set them at opposites, and He formed through them: Three Mothers: Aleph, Mem, Shin in the universe, and Three Mothers: Aleph, Mem, Shin in the year, and Three Mothers: Aleph, Mem, Shin in the body of male and female.

4. Three Mothers: Aleph, Mem, Shin: The product of [elemental] Fire is the Heavens, the product of [elemental] Air is Air, and the product of [elemental] Water is Earth. Fire is above, Water is below, and Air tips the balance between them. From them the Fathers are generated and, from them, everything is created.

5. Three Mothers: Aleph, Mem, Shin are in the universe: Air, Water and Fire: Heavens were created first from [elemental] Fire, Earth was created from [elemental] Water, Air was created from [elemental] Air and it tips the balance between them.

6. Three Mothers: Aleph, Mem, Shin are in the year: Cold, Heat, and Temperate-state: Heat was created from [elemental] Fire, Cold was created from [elemental] Water, Temperate-state was created from [elemental] Air and it tips the balance between them.

7. Three Mothers: Aleph, Mem, Shin are in the body of male and female: Head, Belly, and Chest: Head was created from Fire, Belly was created from Water, Chest was created from Air and it tips the balance between them.

8. He caused the letter Aleph to reign over Air, and
   > He tied a crown to it, and
   > He combined them with one another, and
   > He formed through them:
   >> Air in the universe, and the
   >> Temperate-state in the year, and the
   >> Chest in the body of male with Aleph, Mem, Shin,
   >>> and female with Aleph, Shin, Mem.

Throughout the Sefer Yetsira, the word for "body" is *nefesh*, which is usually translated as "soul." The context here and at the end of the book calls for "body," however.

MISHNA 4: The repetition here is due to manuscript irregularities. I have not always included the explicatory word "[elemental]," so as to give the reader a feeling for the text, but it is always intended.

9. He caused the letter Mem to reign over Water, and
 He tied a crown to it, and
 He combined them with one another, and
 He formed through them:
  Earth in the universe, and
  Cold in the year, and the
  Belly in the body of male with Mem, Aleph, Shin,
   and female with Mem, Shin, Aleph.

10. He caused the letter Shin to reign over Fire, and
 He tied a crown to it, and
 He combined them with one another, and
 He formed through them:
  Heavens in the universe, and
  Heat in the year, and
  Head in the body of male with Shin, Aleph, Mem,
   and female with Shin, Mem, Aleph.

CHAPTER 4

1. Seven double letters: Bet Gimel Dalet, Kaf Pey Resh and Tav, their foundation is Life, Peace, Wisdom, Wealth, Gracefulness, Seed, and Dominion.

2. Seven double letters: Bet Gimel Dalet, Kaf Pey Resh and Tav behave with two sounds: Bet Bhet, Gimel Ghimel, Dalet Dhalet, Kaf Khaf, Pey Phey, Resh Rhesh, Tav Thav, a construction of soft and hard, strong and weak.

3. Seven double letters: Bet Gimel Dalet, Kaf Pey Resh and Tav. are such in speech and as opposites: The opposite of Life is Death. The opposite of Peace is Evil. The opposite of Wisdom is Folly. The opposite of Wealth is Poverty. The opposite of Gracefulness is Ugliness. The opposite of Seed is Desolation. The opposite of Dominion is Slavery.

4. Seven double letters: Bet Gimel Dalet, Kaf Pey Resh and Tav correspond to seven extremities. Six extremities of them are: Above and Below, East and West, North and South. And the Holy Temple is set in the middle and it supports all of them.

MISHNA 1: These are all blessings which are generated from these letters.

MISHNA 2: According to grammatical convention, the first letter of each of these doubles has a dot in it called the "hard dot." Hence, the letter is "hard."

MISHNA 3: Note that the opposite of peace is evil. One manuscript reads "war," but the principle of *lectio difficilior praestat* ("the more difficult reading has precedence") is operative on the grounds that no one would change "war" into "evil," but someone might choose the easy way and emend "evil" into "war." The reading "evil," then, must be the more accurate because it is the more difficult to explain. Actually, the contrast may derive from Isaiah 45:7.

5. Seven double letters: Bet Gimel Dalet, Kaf Pey Resh and Tav seven and not six, seven and not eight, test them and explore them, and understand the matter thoroughly, and restore the Creator to his place.

6. Seven double letters: Bet Gimel Dalet, Kaf Pey Resh and Tav are the foundation. He engraved them, He hewed them out, He combined them, He weighed them, and He set them at opposites, and He formed through them:
   Seven Stars in the universe,
   Seven Days in the year,
   Seven Gates in the body of male and female.
   And from them He engraved seven heavens, and seven earths, and seven Sabbaths. Therefore He cherished the seventh under all the heavens.

7. And these are the Seven Stars in the universe: Sun, Venus, Mercury, Moon, Saturn, Jupiter, Mars. And these are the Seven Days in the year: the seven days of creation. And Seven Gates in the body of male and female: two eyes, two ears, the mouth, and the two apertures of the nose. And through them He engraved seven heavens, and seven earths, and seven hours, therefore He cherished the seventh of every object under the heavens.

8. He caused the letter Bet to reign over Life, and
   He tied a crown to it, and
   He combined them with one another, and
   He formed through them: Saturn in the universe, the first day in the year, and the right eye in the body of male and female.

   He caused the letter Gimel to reign over Peace, and
   He tied a crown to it, and
   He combined them with one another, and

MISHNA 5: Again, the magical testing is referred to.

MISHNA 7: Note which are the "seven stars." This is standard ancient astronomy, with the Earth at the center of the universe and the various heavens revolving around it.

MISHNA 8: The chart for this mishna is as follows:

The double letters	Bet	Gimel	Daled	Kof	Pey	Resh	Tav
the blessing							
the star							
the day of Creation							
the gate of the body							

He formed through them: Jupiter in the universe, the second day in the year, and the left eye in the body of male and female.

He caused the letter Dalet to reign over Wisdom, and
He tied a crown to it, and
He combined them with one another, and
He formed through them: Mars in the universe, the third day in the year, and the right ear in the body of male and female.

He caused the letter Kaf to reign over Wealth, and
He tied a crown to it, and
He combined them with one another, and
He formed through them: Sun in the universe, the fourth day in the year, and the left ear in the body of male and female.

He caused the letter Pey to reign over Gracefulness, and
He tied a crown to it, and
He combined them with one another, and
He formed through them: Venus in the universe, the fifth day in the year, and the right nostril in the body of male and female.

He caused the letter Resh to reign over Seed, and
He tied a crown to it, and
He combined them with one another, and
He formed through them: Mercury in the universe, the sixth day in the year, and the left nostril in the body of male and female.

He caused the letter Tav to reign over Dominion, and
He tied a crown to it, and
He combined them with one another, and
He formed through them: Moon in the universe, the Sabbath day in the year, and the mouth in the body of male and female.

9. Seven double letters: Bet Gimel Dalet, Kaf Pey Resh and Tav through which are engraved seven universes, seven heavens, seven earths, seven seas, seven rivers, seven deserts, seven days, seven weeks, seven years, seven Sabbatical years, seven jubilees, and the Holy

---

MISHNA 9: Every seventh year is a Sabbatical year according to the Bible. Every seventh Sabbatical year is doubly holy, and the fiftieth year of the cycle is called the Jubilee year. Note that here, as in Mishna 4, the Temple serves as a microcosm. Note, too, that if God prefers the seventh of each sequence, then He prefers the Tav (perhaps the mark of Cain), the blessing of Dominion, the Moon, the Sabbath, and the Mouth (which, by the power

Temple. Therefore He cherished the seventh ones under all the heavens.

10. Two stones build two houses,
    Three stones build six houses,
    Four stones build twenty-four houses,
    Five stones build one hundred and twenty houses,
    Six stones build seven hundred and twenty houses,
    Seven stones build five thousand and forty houses.
    From here on go out and think what the mouth is
    unable to speak, and the ear is unable to hear.

---

of speech, creates). The manuscripts, however, differ on the sequence of the blessings, with many ascribing Gracefulness to Tav.

MISHNA 10: The anonymous translator has supplied the following diagram:

2 Stones: AB   BA

3 Stones: ABG   AGB
          BAG   BGA
          GAB   GBA

4 Stones: ABGD   ABDG   AGBD   AGDB   ADBG   ADGB
          BAGD   BADG   BGAD   BGDA   BDAG   BDGA
          GABD   GADB   GBAD   GBDA   GDAB   GDBA
          DABG   DAGB   DBAG   DBGA   DGAB   DGBA

—and so forth . . .

To get the next figure, multiply the sum by the next numeral. For twenty-two letters, the number of permutations is 1,124,000,727,777,607,-680,000 (that's one sextillion . . .). By accumulating the sums, one can calculate the total number of permutations for the usual alphabetic sequence. By varying the alphabetic sequence and then generating a new set of permutations, one does pass beyond comprehensibility. Note, however, that this Jewish creative magic does *not* compel God (as does pagan magic). It has power only over matter and, perhaps, angels.

CHAPTER 5

1. Twelve simple letters: Hey Vav Zayin, Chet Tet Yod, Lamed Nun Samech, Ayin Tzade Kof. Their foundation is sight, hearing, smelling, speaking, tasting, sexual intercourse, work, movement, wrath, laughter, thinking, sleep.

2. Twelve simple letters: Hey Vav Zayin, Chet Tet Yod, Lamed Nun Samech, Ayin Tzade Kof. Their foundation is the twelve borders of a diagonal:
   East-North border, East-South border, East-Above border,
   East-Below border;
   North-Above border, North-Below border;
   West-North border, West-South border, West-
   Above border, West-Below border;
   South-Above border, South-Below border.
   And they continually become wider for ever and ever, and they are the arms of the universe.

3. Twelve simple letters: Hey Vav Zayin, Chet Tet Yod, Lamed Nun Samech, Ayin Tzade Kof. He engraved their foundation, He hewed them out, He combined them, He weighed them, and He set them at opposites, and He formed through them:
   Twelve Constellations in the universe,
   Twelve Months in the year,
   Twelve Organs in the body of male and female.

4. The Twelve Constellations in the universe are: Aries, Taurus, Gemini, Cancer, Leo, Virgo, Libra, Scorpio, Sagittarius, Capricorn, Aquarius, Pisces.

MISHNA 1: These are the twelve activities that characterize man. Again, the manuscripts differ on the sequence.

MISHNA 2: The image here is of a person who is inside a cube which, in turn, is inside a sphere. To picture it more easily, disregard the sphere. Facing in any direction, the person imagines the plane which is parallel with his face. He then imagines this plane intersecting with the perpendicular plane coming at his face-plane from behind, on his right side. Then, from behind, on his left side; then, from behind, above; and then from behind, below. He is, thus, boxed-in in front, on two sides, above, and below by these planes. The lines of intersection are the "borders" of the mishna. As the cube grows to infinity, so do the lines of intersection.

38

5. The Twelve Months in the year are: Nisan, Iyar, Sivan, Tammuz, Av, Elul, Tishri, Cheshvan, Kislev, Tevet, Shevat, Adar.

6. The Twelve Organs in the body of male and female are: two hands, two feet, two kidneys, gall, small intestine, liver, gullet, stomach, spleen.

7. He caused the letter Hey to reign over speech, and He tied a crown to it, and He combined them with one another, and He formed through them: Aries in the universe, and Nisan in the year, and the right foot in the body of male and female.

He caused the letter Vav to reign over thought, and
He tied a crown to it, and
He combined them with one another, and
He formed through them: Taurus in the universe, and Iyar in the year, and the right kidney in the body of male and female.

He caused the letter Zayin to reign over movement, and
He tied a crown to it, and
He combined them with one another, and
He formed through them: Gemini in the universe, and Sivan in the year, and the left foot in the body of male and female.

He caused the letter Chet to reign over sight, and
He tied a crown to it, and
He combined them with one another, and
He formed through them: Cancer in the universe, and Tammuz in the year, and the right hand in the body of male and female.

He·caused the letter Tet to reign over hearing, and
He tied a crown to it, and
He combined them with one another, and
He formed through them: Leo in the universe, and Av in the year, and the left kidney in the body of male and female.

MISHNA 7: The chart for this is as follows:

Letter	Hey	Vav	Zayin	Chet	Tet	Yod	Lamed	Nun	Samech	Ayin	Tzade	Kof
Constellation Month Organ												

The diagram in Figure 8 shows the representation as a sunset, with the letter "AU" being an Aleph. Note that the sunset, wall, and battle images, while representing the same creative process, evoke completely different moods as images.

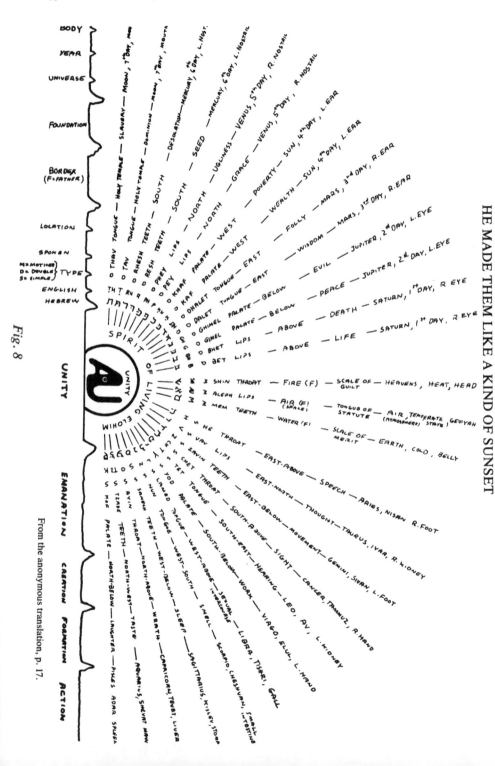

Fig. 8

From the anonymous translation, p. 17.

HE MADE THEM LIKE A KIND OF SUNSET

He caused the letter Yod to reign over work, and
He tied a crown to it, and
He combined them with one another, and
He formed through them: Virgo in the universe, and Elul in the year,
and the left hand in the body of male and female.

He caused the letter Lamed to reign over sexual intercourse, and
He tied a crown to it, and
He combined them with one another, and
He formed through them: Libra in the universe, and Tishri in the year,
and gall in the body of male and female.

He caused the letter Nun to reign over smell, and
He tied a crown to it, and
He combined them with one another, and
He formed through them: Scorpio in the universe, and Cheshvan in the
year, and the small intestines in the body of male and female.

He caused the letter Samech to reign over sleep, and
He tied a crown to it, and
He combined them with one another, and
He formed through them: Sagittarius in the universe, and Kislev in the
year, and the stomach in the body of male and female.

He caused the letter Ayin to reign over wrath, and
He tied a crown to it, and
He combined them with one another, and
He formed through them: Capricorn in the universe, and Tevet in the
year, and the liver in the body of male and female.

He caused the letter Tzade to reign over taste, and
He tied a crown to it, and
He combined them with one another, and
He formed through them: Aquarius in the universe, and Shevat in the
year, and the gullet in the body of male and female.

He caused the letter Kof to reign over laughter, and
He tied a crown to it, and
He combined them with one another, and
He formed through them: Pisces in the universe, and Adar in the year,
and the spleen in the body of male and female.

He made them like a kind of sunset,
He put them in order like a kind of wall,
He set them in order like a kind of battle.

CHAPTER 6

1. These are three Mothers: Aleph, Mem, Shin. There go out from them three Fathers and from the Fathers are Progeny. Three Fathers and their progeny, and seven stars and their hosts, and twelve borders of a diagonal. As proof of the thing are faithful witnesses in the universe, year, body, and the law of the twelve, seven, and three. He assigned them in the Dragon, the Diurnal Sphere, and the Heart.

2. These are three Mothers: Aleph, Mem, Shin—Air, Water, Fire: Fire above, Water below, and Air is that which tips the balance between them. And this is the sign of the thing: the Fire bears the Water. The Mem stands still, the Shin hisses, and the Aleph is Air which tips the balance between them.

3. The Dragon in the universe is like a king on his throne. The Diurnal Sphere in the year is like a king in the province. The Heart in the body is like a king in battle.

MISHNA 1: The original texts here are more obscure than usual. Stenring (*The Book of Formation,* p. 27) lists several mishnayot before this one which summarize the preceding chapters. I have chosen to pick up the narrative at the point of greatest consensus. Note that this is the sixth chapter, corresponding to the sixth day of Creation. The author summarizes the book in several ways and adds three new images: (1) the Dragon—a constellation near the North Star, which swallows the sun and the moon during eclipses, (2) the Diurnal Sphere—the outermost heaven, which rotates once every twenty-four hours and sets the basic rhythm of time, and (3) the Heart—the central organ of the body, which feels and thinks.

Note, too, that nature is a witness, a proof, of the creative order.

MISHNA 2: See above, 1:1.

MISHNA 3: The Dragon rules the material world. The Diurnal Sphere rules time. And the Heart rules the body. The three metaphors are not clear.

4. Also ELOHIM made every object, one opposite the other: good opposite evil, evil opposite good; good from good, evil from evil. The good delineates the evil and the evil delineates the good. Good is kept for the good ones and evil is kept for the evil ones.

5. Three: Each person stands by himself: one acquits, one condemns, and one tips the balance between them. Seven: Three opposite three and one is that which tips the balance between them. Twelve: stand in battle: Three love, three hate, three give life, and three kill.

   Three love: the heart and the ears.

   Three hate: the liver, the gall, and the tongue.

   Three give life: the two apertures of the nose and the spleen.

   Three kill: the two orifices and the mouth.

   And EL, the faithful King, rules over all of them from His Holy Dwelling-place unto Eternity.

   One is above three, three above seven, seven above twelve, and all of them connected with each other. The sign of it is: twenty-two needs in one body.

6. These are the twenty-two letters through which EHEYEH YH, YHVH-ELOHIM, ELOHIM-YHVH, YHVH of Hosts, ELOHIM of Hosts, EL SHADDAI, YHVH-Lord, engraved. And He made from them three principles, and created from them all His universe, and He formed through them everything that is formed, and everything that is destined to be formed.

7. When Abraham our father, may he rest in peace, came: he
   looked, and
   saw, and
   understood, and
   explored, and
   engraved, and
   hewed out, and
   succeeded at Creation as it is said, "And the bodies
   they had made in Haran" [Genesis 12:5].

MISHNA 6: These are some of the combinations of God's various names.

MISHNA 7: The phrase "at Creation as . . ." is in only some manuscripts, but it does confirm that this is a magical text and that the word *nefesh* used here and throughout is intended to mean "living bodies." Note that there are two covenants—one for progeny and one for creative power—and that both the tongue and the male organ can serve as images for either covenant.

The Sefer Yetsira has no real end. Rather, there are all sorts of endings. This indicates that part of the secret of creative power as exercised by God and men was still consciously hidden.

The Lord of All—may His Name be praised forever—was revealed
    to him, and
    He set him in His bosom, and
    He kissed him on his head, and
    He called him "Abraham, my beloved" [Isaiah 41:8], and
    He cut a covenant with him and with his seed forever,
        as it is said "And he believed in YHVH, and He considered
        it to him for righteousness" [Genesis 15:6], and
    He cut a covenant with him between the ten fingers of his hands,
        and that is the covenant of the tongue, and between the ten
        toes of his feet, and that is the covenant of the circum-
        cision, and
    He tied the twenty-two letters of the Torah in his tongue, and
    He revealed to him His secret:
        He drew them through Water,
        He burned them in Fire,
        He shook them through the Air,
        He kindled them in the Seven Stars
        He led them through the twelve constellations.
    [. . .]

Conclusion

Our study of *Ma'aseh Bereshit,* "The Mechanics of Creation," as represented by the Sefer Yetsira has shown us a world which is very strange to modern minds. It is a world founded on intangible beings. It is a world created, and sustained, by animated letters and spiritual "elements." It is a world of strange correlations and of an even stranger cause-effect structure. Yet it definitely has a power and beauty of its own.

By whom and for whom was Sefer Yetsira written? It was written by highly educated orthodox rabbis for other highly educated orthodox rabbis. It was not intended for the masses. It is not written in simple style. In fact, after fifteen centuries of commentation, some of the key passages are still not clear. Why was this book written? It was written as an elucidation of some of the problems of the Genesis Creation story and as an instruction in creative magic.

The Talmud, that great compendium of rabbinic literature, reports many instances of magic as practiced by the rabbis. One example must suffice:

> What [magic] is entirely permitted?
> Such as [the magic] performed by R. Hanina and R. 'Oshaia, who spent every Sabbath eve in studying the Laws of Creation, by means of which they created a third-grown calf and ate it.*

The Talmud does not specify how or why the "Laws of Creation" worked, but the Sefer Yetsira does. Creative magic "worked" for the rabbis because Creation itself was, after the formation of the sefirot and the letters, a mechanical—a magical—process.

By this I mean that God, too, in Creation acted as an artisan who uses his tools and material and who, therewith, "creates" new objects. God used His animated letters and spiritual elements, and once man had the

---

*Talmud, *Sanhedrin* 67a, cited in J. Neusner, *There We Sat Down* (New York and Nashville: Abingdon Press, 1972), p. 80.

knowledge and the spirituality, he too could use the same tools and the same elements to create. Rabbinic magic was not a coercing of God into doing the will of man. It was a parallel, though lesser, use of the same Power. And for that reason, magic was "permitted" within Rabbinic Judaism *only* when practiced by a rabbi, that is, only when the creative act was done with the same spiritual craftsmanship as the original Creative Act. The rabbi, when pious and knowledgeable, shared part of God's Power. That was the "image" of God in which man had been created.

Finally, a study of Sefer Yetsira does yield answers to some, but not all, of the unanswered questions of Genesis. First, Sefer Yetsira clearly states that the "uncreated" elements of the Genesis text all were, in fact, generated at their proper time and place in the unfolding of the universe. Thus, the chaos, the abyss, the waters, the spiritual air, the angels, the darkness, etc., all came into being after Creation had begun. Nothing was co-eternal with God. Second, Sefer Yetsira clearly interprets the "image" of God in which man was created as the power of "hewing and engraving," i.e., the power of Creation itself, on a lesser scale to be sure. Third, Sefer Yetsira interprets the "speech" of God in a very clear way. God did not talk to Himself, like an absolute monarch who wills and it is done. Rather, He generated substance, from which He formed letters, out of which He combined "words," which became things. God's "speech" was not sound but a modeling of units of clay. He is the great Potter here, not the King. Fourth, the gap between God, Who is pure spirit, and Creation, which is matter, is here bridged by the various levels of spiritual matter and spiritual beings. We still do not know how the transition from spirit to matter is accomplished, except that it is done in stages. That is an important contribution (right or wrong) to the understanding of what happened at Creation. And last, Sefer Yetsira does not tell us anything of why God created the world. Although it teaches us some of the secrets of how the universe came to be, Sefer Yetsira still does not tell us why there was a Beginning. Is this a more elegant version than Genesis? Is it more spiritual? And, in the end, do we really know more?

Ma'aseh Bereshit had a complement, *Ma'aseh Merkabah*. This latter term encompassed the visionary, mystical experiences of the rabbis of late antiquity. And it is to that realm of splendor that we turn now.

4

THE VISIONARY ASCENT, PART ONE

Introduction

That Judaism has a nonrepresentational mode of comprehending God has become a truism, but, as with most truisms, it is only partly true. On the one hand, Biblical and Rabbinic Judaism teach that God's transcendence precludes the possibility of depicting Him (cf. the Second Commandment and Deuteronomy 4:12, 15). Yet, on the other hand, there is a well-established tradition of the visible, physical Presence of God. Thus, for example, Exodus 16:10 reports: "While Aaron was speaking to the community of Israelites, they turned toward the desert and behold the *Kavod* of God had descended in a cloud." Similarly, at other crucial moments in Moses' career, the *Kavod* of God appeared (Exodus 24:16 and Numbers 14:10, 16:19, 20:6). Furthermore, at the completion of the Tabernacle in the desert and again at the completion of the Solomonic Temple in Jerusalem, the *Kavod* of God came to fill the sanctuary (Leviticus 9:23, with I Kings 8:11 and II Chronicles 5:14; 7:2). It is also the case that the Bible reports angels, cherubs, seraphs, and other heavenly hosts (cf., e.g., Isaiah 6). The Psalms, too, some of which were written on (or for) the pilgrimage, speak of visions of God (Psalm 63:3), of God's *Kavod* (Psalm 24), and of similar visual representations of the divine. There is, thus, a component within Biblical tradition which recognizes such theophanies as legitimate, and, as we shall see, there is a distinct representational imagination at work in the rabbinic literature as well.

Perhaps the two most startling visual appearances of God in the Bible are those described at the beginning of the Book of Ezekiel and in chapter 6 of Isaiah. In the former, the prophet, who is in exile in Babylon, is seized forcibly by God and transported to the flat plains of the Euphrates Valley. As he looks up, he sees a vision approaching him and begins to describe it. It is the *Kavod* of God, and this theophany constitutes the inaugural vision of the prophet although the *Kavod* will be seen by him again (see Ezekiel 8, 10, and 11).

What exactly did the prophet see? To understand what the prophet saw, the reader must remember the Ezekiel is describing something which is approaching him. Hence, the descriptions tend to be repetitive, but with more detail each time. Furthermore, because this is a visual, and not an auditory, manifestation, the reader is well advised to try to sketch it. Begin with the "vault of the awesome color of ice." The reader, with or without his own sketch, must ask: What are these heavenly beings? Why do the four Hayot ("Creatures") have the faces they do? How many eyes does each Hayah have? Why do the Ofannim ("Wheels") have eyes? And, generally, what is the impression this vision makes? Most important though: Is this a mystic vision? And, if not, why not? Do the same with chapter 6 of Isaiah: What are the Seraphim ("Fiery Beings")? Is that vision a recounting of a mystic experience, and if not, why not?

Ezekiel's Vision

On the fifth day of the fourth month in the thirtieth year, while I was among the exiles by the river Kebar, the heavens were opened and I saw a vision of God. On the fifth day of the month in the fifth year of the exile of King Jehoiachin, the word of the LORD came to Ezekiel son of Buzi the priest, in Chaldea, by the river Kebar, and there the hand of the Lord came upon him.

I saw a storm wind coming from the north, a vast cloud with flashes of fire and brilliant light about it; and within was a radiance like brass, glowing in the heart of the flames. In the fire was the semblance of four living creatures in human form. Each had four faces and each four wings; their legs were straight, and their hooves were like the hooves of a calf, glittering like a disc of bronze. Under the wings on each of the four sides were human hands; all four creatures had faces and wings, and their wings touched one another. They did not turn as they moved; each creature went straight forward. Their faces were like this: all four had the face of a man and the face of a lion on the right, on the left the face of an ox and the face of an eagle. Their wings were spread; each living creature had one pair touching its neighbours', while one pair covered its body. They moved straight forward in whatever direction the spirit would go; they never swerved in their course. The appearance of the creatures was as if fire from burning coals or torches were darting to and fro among them; the fire was radiant, and out of the fire came lightning.

As I looked at the living creatures, I saw wheels on the ground, one beside each of the four. The wheels sparkled like topaz, and they were all alike: in form and working they were like a wheel inside a wheel, and when they moved in any of the four directions they never swerved in their course. All four had hubs and each hub had a projection which had the power of sight, and the rims of the wheels were full of eyes all round. When the living creatures moved, the wheels moved beside them; when the creatures rose from the ground, the wheels rose; they moved in whatever direction the spirit would go; and the wheels rose together with them, for the spirit of the living creatures was in the wheels. When the one moved, the other moved;

From *The New English Bible,* pp. 1005–6.

when the one halted, the other halted; when the creatures rose from the ground, the wheels rose together with them, for the spirit of the creatures was in the wheels.

Above the heads of the living creatures was, as it were, a vault glittering like a sheet of ice, awe-inspiring, stretched over their heads above them. Under the vault their wings were spread straight out, touching one another, while one pair covered the body of each. I heard, too, the noise of their wings; when they moved it was like the noise of a great torrent or of a cloud-burst, like the noise of a crowd or of an armed camp; when they halted their wings dropped. A sound was heard above the vault over their heads, as they halted with drooping wings. Above the vault over their heads there appeared, as it were, a sapphire in the shape of a throne, and high above all, upon the throne, a form in human likeness. I saw what might have been brass glowing like fire in a furnace from the waist upwards; and from the waist downwards I saw what looked like fire with encircling radiance. Like a rainbow in the clouds on a rainy day was the sight of that encircling radiance; it was like the appearance of the glory of the LORD.

When I saw this I threw myself on my face, and heard a voice speaking to me . . .

Conclusion

The vision of Ezekiel contains images of two types of heavenly hosts: the Hayot (sing. Haya), or Creatures, and the Ofannim (sing. Ofan), or Wheels. Each Hayah stands erect, has a torso and a pedestal of burnished copper, covers its body with some of its wings, "flies" with the other wings, and each has one head with four faces, representing the head of each kingdom (the eagle of the birds, the lion of the beasts, the ox of the domesticated animals, and man—according to other texts, a cherub—of the intelligent beings). The Ofannim are sets of two gigantic wheels, intersecting at right angles, which are also intelligent (i.e., they have eyes). In the midst, lightning; around the vision, radiance. The divine Presence (the Figure on the Throne) is seen. The impression is one of awe and transcendence, and the prophet, realizing this, prostrates himself.

Ezekiel's vision (like Isaiah's) is not, however, a mystic vision. It is nothing that the prophet has sought. It is nothing he has built up to by intellectual preparation and spiritual discipline. Rather, it is God Who has seized the prophet and overwhelmed him with His majesty. Furthermore, there is no "unification" of the prophet with God and no secret knowledge conveyed. Rather, the prophet has felt humbled, and the communication he has received is an ethical message for the people, a preachment.

And yet the prophet has been given a glimpse (as has Isaiah) of what life is like "up there." He has been allowed a quick look at some members of the heavenly hosts. The heavens have, indeed, been opened for him, for a short time. Ezekiel has seen more than others, or at least he has described what he has seen in greater detail than anyone else. His vision is shockingly precise. And it is exactly this explicitness that caused later mystics to ponder this chapter and to extrapolate it to new and greater heights. This chapter, known to Ezekiel as the *Kavod,* became central to later Jewish mystical tradition, and there it is known as the *Merkabah.* This theophany, describing God's "Chariot," became the goal of the mystical efforts of the rabbis, and it is to that effort and the literature it produced that we now turn.

5

THE VISIONARY ASCENT, PART TWO

Introduction

The term in Rabbinic Judaism for the theme of mysticism is *Ma'aseh Merkabah,* which is best translated as "The Labor of the Vision" or "The Mechanics of the Vision." It is a term which encompasses very precise knowledge about the workings of the supernal world as well as precise indications of how the mystic is to arrive at, and behave in, that realm. As with *Ma'aseh Bereshit,* the *Ma'aseh Merkabah* was kept very secret, and as a result, only fragments have come down to us. One such fragment is presented here, the *Pirkei Heikhalot,* or *Chapters on Ascent.* (For the background to this and other such material, see chap. 1 above, "Doctrinal Summary," and the sources cited there.) Before beginning the study of this text, we must know something of its context, its purpose, and its structure.

Pirkei Heikhalot, like Sefer Yetsira, has three important contexts. First, there is the Biblical context, for Pirkei Heikhalot existed within the framework of the great theophanic passages of Biblical literature, such as Ezekiel 1. Every glimpse of the heavenly court recorded in the Bible became a springboard into the heavenly realm of the Merkabah literature. Second, there is the context of late antiquity, for the Pirkei Heikhalot is replete with concepts and ideas that are common to that milieu. Thus, the plethora of heavenly beings, the use of name-seals, and the dangers of the ascent are all central ideas here as in the parallel literature of late antiquity. Some scholarly work has been done on this, and more remains to be done. And third, both these contexts are filtered through the rabbinic world-view, which conceived all of reality as ordered by the will of the single, transcendent God as embodied in His Torah.

The purposes of the Pirkei Heikhalot are two: to describe the kingdom of the heavenly hosts, and to instruct the mystic on the proper approach to the King. It is important to note in this respect that the editor (or editors) of this text justified the revelation of these secrets because they felt that the continuity of the esoteric chain was threatened by persecution. It became important, then, to commit it to writing.

Given these contexts and these purposes, there are many questions to be asked. First, by whom and for whom was this text written? Who would write or read it, and why? And how would such a person use this text? Second, why are there so many angels? What do we learn from their names? Which groups appear more powerful? How does the mystic counteract their power? What are the danger points in the ascent, and why are there such points? Third, concerning the mystical experience itself (as reported in the text): What preparations are necessary? What type of experience is it? What does the mystic say he experiences? What does he report that he hears? sees? What do the heavenly hymns convey as a literary genre? And fourth, we want to bear in mind the general questions of this whole unit: What are the characteristics of this material? What kind of impression does it make on the reader? And what motivated this kind of text? What sensitivities and feelings lie behind it? What is its secret?

The structure of the Pirkei Heikhalot is as follows:

Chaps. 15 and 16 — the "historical" justification for revealing the Way and the prerequisites for mystic ascent

Chaps. 17 and 18 — the list of the names of the angels and an adumbration of ecstasy

Chap. 19:1–5 — instructions for passage through the gates of the first five palaces

Chap. 19:6–20:4 — excursus on the dangers of the gates of the sixth palace

Chap. 20:5–22:1 — instructions for passage through the gates of the sixth palace

Chap. 22:2–3 — passage through the gates of the seventh palace

Chap. 22:4–24:2 — excursus on the dangers of the gates of the seventh palace

Chap. 24:3–25 — ecstasy

Chap. 26:1–2 — dangers

Chap. 26:3–28:4 — further hymns

Chap. 28:5–29:5 — the beginning of God's response to the mystic

A word about the text as presented here: It is a translation of chapters 15–29 of the *Heikhalot Rabbati,* based on the edition of S. A. Wertheimer in his *Batei Midrashot* (Jerusalem: Mossad Harav Kook, 1968), vol. 1, pp. 90–114. The translation was prepared by Ms. Lauren Grodner and was edited and annotated by me. The following sections have been adapted, with changes, from other translations: 15:1 from M. Smith, "Observations on *Hekhalot Rabbati,*" in *Biblical and Other Studies,* ed. A. Altmann

(Cambridge: Harvard University Press, 1963), p. 144; 17:8–18:2 from G. Scholem, *Jewish Gnosticism, Merkabah Mysticism, and Talmudic Tradition* New York: Jewish Theological Seminary, 1965), pp. 31–32; 20:2–3 from ibid., p. 11; 24:1 from ibid., p. 62; 28:1 from Scholem, *Major Trends in Jewish Mysticism,* pp. 58–59. The essays listed above provide a great deal of the background to this material, although a full scholarly study of this material remains to be done. The world of scholarship looks forward eagerly to the scholarly translation and annotation of the entire *Heikhalot Rabbati* by M. Smith. Other materials from this period include *The Visions of Ezekiel* being prepared by L. Jacobs.

Pirkei Heikhalot: Text and Commentary

Translated by L. Grodner, edited by D. Blumenthal

CHAPTER 15

1. Rabbi Ishmael said, When R. Nehunya ben Hakkanah saw Rome was planning to destroy the mighty of Israel, he at once revealed the secret of the world as it appears to one who is worthy to gaze on the King and His Throne in His majesty and His beauty: [upon] the Hayot of holiness, the Cherubim of might, and the Wheels of the Shekhina [which are] as lightning mixed with awesome electrum; [upon] the beauty which is around the Throne; [upon] the bridges and the growing chains which rise between the bridges; [upon] the dust, smoke, and the wind which raises the dust of the coals for it conceals and covers all the chambers of the place of Aravot-Raqi'a with the clouds of its coals; and [upon] Surya, the Prince of the Presence, the servant of Totarkhiel-YHVH, the proud one.

MISHNA 1: This mishna sets the stage for the revelations which will follow. Note that the author (or authors) uses the images from Ezekiel. *Aravot* and *Raqi'a* are two Biblical terms referring loosely to some part of heaven. Here they are telescoped into one term and are understood as referring to the highest of the heavens. This meaning of the term remained, although the place designated by it changed in later Jewish tradition. The "mighty" here are the Sages. The "chains" are tongues of fire. R. stands for "Rabbi."

The historical setting chosen by the author is that of the Roman persecutions of the Jews in the years 120–135 C.E. Modern scholars do not usually accept this as the actual date of these texts.

One more important note is sounded here: The angels are divided into two "families"—that of Surya, and they will be called Angels of the Presence, and that of Totarkhiel, and they will have the Tetragrammaton (YHVH) appended to their names. This becomes important later on.

2. What is it like [to know the secret of Merkabah]? It is like having a ladder in one's house [and being able to go up and down at will. This is possible] for anyone who is purged and pure of idolatry, sexual offenses, bloodshed, slander, vain oaths, profanation of the Name, impertinence, and unjustified enmity, and who keeps every positive and negative commandment.

3. R. Ishmael said, R. Nehunya ben Hakkanah said to me: Son of the Proud Ones, happy is he and happy is the soul of everyone who is purged and pure of those eight vices, for Totarkhiel-YHVH, and Surya his servant despise them.

4. He who "goes down" looks with a wondrous proudness and a strange powerfulness, with the proudness of exultation and the powerfulness of radiance, for these [two emotions] are stirred up before the Throne of His Glory [three] times each day, on high, ever since the world was created until now, to praise [Him], for Totarkhiel-YHVH acts thus on high.

MISHNA 2: The requirements are very rabbinic and involve moral purity, ritual obedience, and, by implication, study or intellectual ability. Note, no women allowed.

MISHNA 3: The "Proud Ones" (Heb. *Ben Ge'im*) is a term which refers to the practitioners of this type of mysticism, i.e., to the initiated. Note that even Totarkhiel-YHVH is one of them. The meaning is that the initiated and the angels share in the majestic pride that God has in His Creation. The word "proud," thus, has no pejorative moral overtones. Does the phrase "Six for the six proud walkers" of the popular English folksong "Green Grow the Rushes, Ho" refer to some such mystical group?

MISHNA 4: This mishna repeats itself, and it has a wonderful rhythm which is difficult to catch. The reference to "three times each day" is a reference to the number of times that prayers (praises) are recited in heaven, and this number parallels the number of times that a Jew prays each day.

To "go down" is a strange and perplexing term, especially when taken with 23:2; 23:4; 2:3, and 16:4, where the term "go up" also occurs. There are several possibilities: (1) The terms are purposeful double-talk, a phenomenon not unusual in mystic literature. (2) The terms have no special mystical meaning, and, indeed, they are common verbs meaning "to go" in rabbinic Hebrew. (3) They are mystical nuances to the two usual liturgical terms "to go down to the prayerstand [and lead the congregation in prayer]" and "to go up to the [ritual] reading of the Torah." (4) One term means to ascend the mystical ladder, and the other to descend. And (5), some mystical techniques are meant—either breathing techniques or meditational techniques for gaining "mystical space" by turning inward/outward. No one knows for sure.

CHAPTER 16

1. R. Ishmael said, When my ears had heard this warning, my strength ebbed and I said to him: My Rabbi, If this is so, there is no end to the matter, for there is no man in possession of a soul who is so purged and pure of these eight vices. He then said to me: Son of the Proud Ones, perhaps not. Go and bring before me all the courageous members of the group *(havura)* and all the mighty ones of the academy *(yeshiva)* so that I may recite in their presence the secrets and mysteries which have been suppressed, [the] wonders and the weaving of the tractate upon which the betterment of the world, the setting (of the world) on its path, and the beautification of heaven and earth depend, for all the ends of the earth and the universe and the ends of the upper heavens are bound, sewn, and connected, dependent upon it [i.e., the secret knowledge]. And the path of the heavenly ladder whose one end is on earth and whose other end is in heaven at the right foot of the Throne of Glory [depend on it too].

2. R. Ishmael said, I immediately went and gathered together every great and small Sanhedrin to the great third entrance of the House of God. I sat on a bench of pure marble which my father, Elisha, had given me from the estate of my mother, who had so stipulated in her marriage contract.

MISHNA 1: Here we have the classic statement of what a "gnosis" is: It is a secret knowledge. Its content is the system by which the whole cosmos is put together. And by proper use of it ("praxis"), the universe can be manipulated and even put into better order. Note that the *havura* is the mystic fellowship composed of an inner elite of the Sages. The modern use of the term *havura* to denote "a religious fellowship" has its roots here. For the ladder, see Genesis 28:12.

MISHNA 2: "Sanhedrin" is a court. The "House of God" is the Temple, and since it had been destroyed, R. Ishmael means that he gathered everyone to the spot where the third gate had stood. Was the Jerusalem setting just a literary device? Even if so, the scene was still impressive.

3. Then, the [following men] came: Rabban Shimon b. Gamliel, R. Eliezer Ha-gadol, R. Elazar b. Damah, R. Eliezer b. Shamua, R. Yohanan b. Dahavai, Hananya b. Chanichai, Yonathan b. Uziel, R. Akiba, and R. Judah b. Baba. We [all] came and sat before him while the mass of companions (*haverim*) stood on their feet, for they saw that globes of fire and torches of light formed a barrier between them and us. R. Nehunya ben Hakkanah sat and set in order for them [i.e., the whole group] all the matters of the Merkabah: the descent to it and the ascent, how to descend, who should descend, how to ascend, and who should ascend.

4. When anyone would want to "go down to the Chariot" he would call upon Surya, the Angel of the Presence, and make him swear [to protect him] one hundred and twelve times in the name of Tootruseah-YHVH who is called Tootruseah Tzortak Totarkhiel Tofgar Ashrooleah Zevoodiel and Zeharariel Tandiel Shoked Hoozeah Dahivoorin and Adiriron-YHVH, Lord of Israel.

MISHNA 3: These men could all have sat together. On the meanings of ascend and descend, see 1:4. The "globes of fire and torches of light" are supernatural phenomena which divide the elite of the elite from the others.

MISHNA 4: For the meaning of this oath, see the next mishna. A whole book could be written about the meaning of the names of the angels. I shall comment on only three names. The name Tootruseah is composed of the Greek word for "four"—*tetra* (referring to the four-letter Name of God, YHVH, known as the Tetragrammaton)—plus the Greek word for "essence" or "being"—*ousion*. It is, thus, a compound word meaning "the essence of the four-[lettered Name]." Similarly, the name Totarkhiel is composed of *tetra* plus the Hebrew word *'EL* (which is one of the powerful names of God). The *kh* sound is for phonetic purposes. To Totarkhiel the YHVH is usually appended. The name Zeharariel is composed of two Hebrew elements—*zohar*, meaning "radiance," and *'El* (one of the powerful names of God), plus an additional *r* for phonetic reasons. These angel names, then, (1) usually have a divine element added to them, (2) often are composed of Greek and/or Hebrew elements. Some of them, however, are completely obscure.

5. He may not do it more than one hundred and twelve times, or less, for he who adds or subtracts has his blood on his own head. Rather one's mouth brings forth the names and one's fingers count one hundred and twelve times. He then immediately goes down and [successfully] masters the Merkabah.

MISHNA 5: The mystical ascent is a very dangerous procedure. A misused name would cause the cosmos to be modified in some inopportune way since the Names are creative forces, as we saw in Sefer Yetsira. Furthermore, the heavenly realm is one of great purity and cannot be lightly breached. The practitioner, then, must cause Surya, a very powerful angel, to swear to protect him during the ascent. That oath is the subject of these two mishnayot.

There are seven palaces with eight guards each (four on each side of the gate) = 56 names of the guards of the gates. Since the mystic must ascend and descend, there are 112 guards whose power must be neutralized. Hence, the mystic must administer 112 oaths to Surya.

How was this done? The text does not say. Perhaps the mystic said something like: "I adjure you, Surya, Angel of the Presence, to protect me from the power of . . . ," changing the name each time. It is possible, but not likely, that the mystic simply repeated the full set of Surya's names over and over. That kind of technique is well known in mystical circles but it is used to induce a trance. Here, an oath of protection is administered. Note, though, that upon completing the oath, the mystic does enter a trance ("successfully masters the Merkabah").

CHAPTER 17

1. R. Ishmael said: Thus said R. Nehunya ben Hakkanah: Tootrusea-YHVH, Lord of Israel, dwells in seven palaces, in the innermost room thereof. At the gates of each palace, there are eight guardians: four to the right and four to the left.

2. And these are the names of the guards of the gates of the first palace: Dehaviel, Kashriel, Gahoriel, Botiel, Tofhiel, Dehariel, Matkiel, Shuiel, and some say Sheviel.

3. And these are the names of the guards of the gates of the second palace: Tagriel, Matpiel, Sarhiel, Arfiel, Sheharariel, Satriel, Regaiel, and Saheviel.

4. And these are the names of the guards of the gates of the third palace: Shevooriel, Retzutziel, Shulmooiel, Savliel, Zehazahiel, Hadariel, and Bezariel.

5. And these are the names of the guards of the gates of the fourth palace: Pachdiel, Gevoortiel, Kazooiel, Shekhiniel, Shatkiel, Araviel, Kafiel, and Anaphiel.

6. And these are the names of the guards of the gates of the fifth palace: Tachiel, Uziel, Gatiel, Getahiel, Safriel, Garafiel, Gariel, Dariel, and Falatriel.

MISHNA 1: No one truly knows how to read the names which follow for two reasons: (1) the manuscripts do not agree on the spelling, and (2) written Hebrew has very few vowels. The rendering here is as close as the translator and I can come. As noted above, some have meaning and some do not.

MISHNA 4: There are only seven names here and there should be eight. Conversely, in mishna 6 there is one name too many.

7. And these are the names of the guards of the gates of the sixth palace: Roomiel, Katzmiel, Gehaghiel, Arsavrasbiel, Agroomiel, Faratziel, Mechakiel, and Tofariel.

8. At the gate of the seventh palace, they stand angry and war-like, strong, harsh, fearful, terrifying, taller than mountains and sharper than peaks. Their bows are strung and stand before them. Their swords are sharpened and in their hands. Bolts of lightning flow and issue forth from the balls of their eyes, and balls of fire [issue] from their nostrils, and torches of fiery coals from their mouths. They are equipped with helmets and with coats of mail, and javelins and spears are hung upon their arms.

MISHNA 8: These are the fiercest guards. Note that R. Nehunya did not give the *names* of the guards of the gates of the seventh palace. This sets the stage for 22:4–23:4.

CHAPTER 18

1. The horses upon which they ride stand beside mangers of fire, full of coals of juniper, and they eat fiery coals from the mangers, [taking] a measure of forty bushels of coals in one mouthful. And the measure of the mouth of each horse is as three mangers, such as a manger of Caesarea, and the measure of each manger is as the measure of the gate of Caesarea.

2. There are rivers of fire beside the mangers and their horses drink the measure of the fullness of the water-pipe which is in the Valley of Kidron, which brings and contains all the rain water of all Jerusalem. And there is a cloud over their heads which drips blood [into the air] above the heads of the horses and the guards. This is the sign and the measure of the guards of the seventh palace and of the horses of each of the other gates of each of the palaces.

3. All those who go up to the Merkabah are not harmed even though they see this entire [set of] palaces. And they descend in peace, returning and standing up to testify to the awesome, terrifying sight they have seen, the like of which cannot be seen in any of the palaces of flesh and blood. They, then, bless, praise, extol, exalt, laud, and give glory, tribute, greatness to Tootrusea-YHVH, Lord of Israel, who rejoices with those who descend to the Merkabah. [Indeed,] he sits and waits for each and every Israelite when he comes down in wondrous proudness and in strange powerfulness, a proudness of exultation and the powerfulness of radiance as these are aroused before the Throne of Glory three times daily, in heaven, from Creation until now to sing His praise [to]:

MISHNA 1: "Manger of Caesarea" refers to the stables of the Roman legate to Judaea, the most impressive stables in the country. The heavenly horses, however, exceeded those of the Roman officials. The "gate of Caesarea" is the gate to the imperial city. The next mishna refers to the aqueduct of the city of Jerusalem.

4. The King who is direct; faithful King, beloved King, beautiful King, supportive King, the King who is hurt [by the sins of men], modest King, righteous King, pious King, holy King, pure King, blessed King, proud King, courageous King, gracious King, merciful King, the King of the king of kings.

5. And the Master of the Crowns yearns and waits for Tootrusea-YHVH, Lord of Israel, as he yearns for the Redemption and the time of Salvation that is stored up for Israel following the destruction of the Second, the last, Temple. [He also yearns for] those who go down to the Merkabah when they go down, when they see the exultation on High, when they hear the Salvation of the End, when they see that which no eye sees, and when they reascend to tell the seed of Abraham, his lover, [what they have seen and heard].

CHAPTER 19

1. R. Ishmael said: When you come and stand at the gate of the first palace, take two seals, one in each hand—[the seals] of Tootrusea-YHVH, Lord of Israel, and of Surya, the Angel of the Presence. Show the seal of Tootrusea-YHVH, Lord of Israel, to those who stand on the right, and [the seal] of Surya to those on the left. Then, Bahbiel—the angel who is in charge of the gate of the first palace, is appointed over the palace [itself], and who stands on the right—and Tofhiel—the angel who stands to the left of the threshold—grab you [the initiate], give you peace, and send you forth with radiance (*mashlimin u-mazhirin 'alekha*) to Tagriel, the angel who is in charge of the gate of the second palace and who stands to the right of its threshold, and to Matpiel, who stands with him to the left of its threshold.

2. Show them, then, two seals—one of Adriharon-YHVH, Lord of Israel, and one of Ouzia, the Angel of the Presence. Show the one of Adriharon to the [guards] standing on the right and the one of Ouzia, the Angel of the Presence, show to those [guards] standing on the left. Immediately, they grab you—one on your right and one on your left—as they accompany you, hand you over, give you peace, and send you forth with radiance to Shevooriel, the angel who is in charge of the gate to the third palace, and who stands on its right threshold, and Retzutziel, the angel who stands with him on its left threshold.

MISHNA 1: This chapter contains the instructions for passage through the gates of the first five palaces. In each case, a seal from the "YHVH, Lord of Israel" family is shown to the guards on the right, and a seal from the "Angel of the Presence" family is shown to the guards on the left. The guards are impressed. They cause radiance to descend upon the initiate and send him on to the next gate. Things get more complicated at the gate to the sixth palace. Note well that R. Nehunya is talking in his trance and that the initiate must know all the names and requisite seals before "starting out."

66

3. Show them, then, two seals—one of Tzoortak-YHVH, Lord of Israel and one of Dehavyoron, the Angel of the Presence. Show the one of Tzoortak-YHVH, Lord of Israel, to the [guards] standing on the right, and the one of Dehavyoron, the Angel of the Presence, show to those [guards] standing on your left. Immediately, they grab you, one on your right and one on your left, and they cause two angels to march in front of you and two in back of you. They give you peace and send you forth with radiance to Pahdiel, the angel who is in charge of the gate to the fourth palace, and who stands on its right threshold, and Gevoortiel, the angel who stands with him on its left threshold.

4. Show them, then, two seals—one of Zvoodiel-YHVH, Lord of Israel, and one of Margeyoiel, the Angel of the Presence. Show the one of Zvoodiel to the [guards] standing on the right and the one of Margeyoiel, the Angel of the Presence, show to those [guards] standing on the left. Immediately, they grab you, one on your right and one on your left, as they accompany you, hand you over, give you peace, and send you forth with radiance to Tahiel, the angel who is in charge of the gate to the fifth palace, and who stands on its right threshold, and Uziel, the angel who stands with him on its left threshold.

5. Show them, then two seals—one of Totarviel-YHVH, Lord of Israel, and one of Zahpeniriya, the Angel of the Presence. Show the one of Totarviel-YHVH, Lord of Israel, to the [guards] standing on the right, and the one of Zahpeniriya, the Angel of the Presence, show to those [guards] standing on the left. Immediately, they grab you, three angels in front of you and three angels behind you, [as they accompany you, hand you over, give you peace, and send you forth with radiance to Roomiel, the angel who is in charge of the gate to the sixth palace, and who stands on its right threshold, and Katzmiel, the angel who stands with him on its left threshold].

6. Now, the guards of the sixth palace make a practice of killing those who "go and do not go down to the Merkabah without permission." They hover over them, strike them, and burn them. Others are set in in their place and others in their place [and the same thing happens]. The mentality [of those who are killed] is that they are not afraid nor

---

MISHNA 3: The movement here turns into a procession and continues to get more complicated as the passage goes on.

MISHNA 6: From here to 20:4 is the description of the dangers of the passage through the sixth palace. Rabbi Nehunya tells of the danger rather

do they question: "Why are we being burned?" [The mentality of the guards is that they do not ask:] "What profit do we have that we kill those who go and do not go down to the Merkabah without permission?" Nevertheless, such is the mentality of the guards of the sixth palace.

---

cryptically, and in the next chapter, the men who are learning the secrets from him decide to recall him from the trance to have him explain what he means.

CHAPTER 20

1. Rabbi Ishmael said: The members of the *Havura,* then, said to me: Son of the Proud Ones, you are as much a master of the light of Torah as R. Nehunya ben Hakkanah. See if you can bring him back from the visions which he has glimpsed to sit with us and to tell us the difference between "those who go down to the Merkabah" and "those who go and do not go down to the Merkabah without permission," such that the guards of the gate of the sixth palace strike down the latter but do not touch the former at all. What is the difference between them?

MISHNA 1: Puzzled by R. Nehunya's remark, the members ask R. Ishmael to recall him. The problem is how to do it, and there are two principles acting here: (1) Contact with impurity will render R. Nehunya impure, thus terminating the trance. And (2) to become grossly impure would cause a sudden and violent termination, thus endangering R. Nehunya's life. The rabbi-mystics must, then, design a way to render him impure, but only in the very slightest degree. (I am indebted to my colleague L. Schiffman for the analysis here although Scholem has touched upon it in *Jewish Gnosticism,* p. 10.)

The rabbinic rule is as follows: A menstruating woman is impure. At the end of her period, she must bathe ritually. If she has doubts about her purity, she may check to see if there is still some blood present by wrapping a cloth around her finger and inserting it. If it stains, she is still impure.

The case described in mishna 2 is the subtlest possible case. The woman has stopped menstruating. She has bathed ritually once but, for technical reasons, must do it again. She bathes ritually a second time and is, thus, ritually pure. This woman is then asked to "check" herself but to do it very gently. No trace of staining is found—i.e., she is still pure. But one very, very strict rabbi might still claim she is impure because of possible irregularities in her menstrual cycle. We have, thus, a woman who is ritually pure except in the remotest sense of the word, and we have an object (the cloth) which is ritually impure in the very least degree possible. R. Nehunya, upon touching it, thus becomes as minimally impure as possible.

69

2. Immediately I took a piece of very fine woolen cloth and gave it to R. Akiba, and R. Akiba gave it to a servant of ours saying: Go and lay this cloth beside a woman who immersed herself and yet had not become pure, and let her immerse herself [a second time]. For if that woman will come and will declare the circumstances of her menstrual flow before the company, there will be one who forbids [her to her husband] and the majority will permit. Say to that woman: Touch this cloth with the end of the middle finger of your hand, and do not press the end of your finger upon it, but rather as a man who takes a hair which had fallen therein from his eyeball, pushing it very gently.

3. They went and did so, and laid the cloth before R. Ishmael. He inserted into it a bough of myrtle, full of oil, that had been soaked in pure balsam, and they placed it upon the knees of R. Nehunya ben Hakkanah. Immediately they dismissed him from before the Throne of Glory where he had been sitting and beholding:
    A wondrous proudness and a strange powerfulness,
    A proudness of exaltation and a powerfulness of radiance,
    Which are stirred up before the Throne of Glory,
    Three times each day, in the height,
    From the time the world was created and until now, for praise.

4.· Then we asked him: Who are those who are among those who descend to the Merkabah and [who are] those who are not? He said to us, Those [who "go and do not go down to the Merkabah"] are the men whom those who do go down take with them, whom they then establish above and in front of them, and to whom they say, "Look carefully, see, hear,

---

To further protect R. Nehunya several magical items and acts are performed (mishna 3): From other rabbinic texts we know that certain oils and balsam were said to be poured over the initiate by the angels in order to purify him for his final vision. Similarly, myrtle boughs were used as "magical wands." Knowing this, R. Ishmael takes the cloth, which is impure only in a minimal way, and inserts it into a purifying, protective case. He thus minimizes the impurity further and, hence, affords R. Nehunya even greater protection. R. Nehunya is dismissed and answers the question.

MISHNA 4: The answer is that the mystic can "take along" others and it is they who are in danger at the gate of the sixth palace because they are not genuine mystics. Who are these others? M. Smith ("Observations on *Hekhalot Rabbati*," p. 154) has suggested that they are secretaries who, by some group-mysticism, have been "brought along," and whose job it is to

and write all that I say and all that we hear in the presence of the Throne of Glory." These men, if they are not worthy of the task, are those who are attacked by the guards of the sixth palace. Be cautious, therefore, to choose men who are fit and tested *haverim*.

5. When you come and stand before the gate of the sixth palace, show the three seals of the guards of the sixth palace to Katspiel, the prince, whose sword is unsheathed in his hand. From it lightning shoots outward, and he raises it against anyone who is not worthy to gaze upon the King and His Throne. And there is no creature who can stop him. His drawn sword shouts: "Destruction and annihilation are on the threshold of the right."

6. And [show one seal to] Dumiel. Is Dumiel really his name? Is not Abir Gahidariham his name? Why is he called Dumiel? Rabbi Ishmael said: Thus said R. Nehunya ben Hakkanah: Every day, the echo of a voice goes forth from the uppermost of the heavens and announces: The heavenly court has said: Te'om bar Mautsa Zapokhe Gashash Ga'ashot-YHVH, Lord of Israel, call him Dumiel with My name [in his] for, as I see and am silent, so Dumiel is my agent on the threshold of the right and with him is Katspiel and he bears him no hatred, enmity, jealousy, and competitiveness. Rather, both are for My glory.

---

record what transpires. After his answer, R. Nehunya goes back into his trance and continues his narrative.

MISHNA 5: We seem to have two versions of what happens at the gate of the sixth palace. The first version (20:5–21:2) seems to be the usual showing of the seals plus the presentation of a gift. The second version (21:3–22:1) seems to indicate that a heavenly quizzing of the initiate took place. Perhaps it is only one version poorly told. For our purposes, it does not matter.

MISHNA 6: Scholem (*Jewish Gnosticism,* p. 33) has explained that the longer name is a combination of Greek words but that Dumiel is a Hebrew name, meaning literally "the silence of God" and referring to the mystical silence.

CHAPTER 21

1. Someone should show these two seals of Zoharariel and the works of his works to Katspiel. And show Baroniya to Dumiel, the prince—the prince who is direct and is hurt [by the sins of men]. Immediately, Katspiel, the prince, puts up his bow and sheathes his sword and brings for you a great storm wind. He seats you in a wagon of radiance and he blows the equivalent of eight thousand myriad horns, three thousand myriad *shofarot,* and four thousand myriad trumpets. Dumiel, the prince, takes the [special] gift and goes before you.

2. What is the [special] gift? Rabbi Ishmael said: Thus said R. Nehunya ben Hakkanah, my teacher: The gift which Dumiel, the prince, holds before the wagon of the man who is worthy to go down to the Merkabah is not a gift of silver or of gold. Rather, they [the guards] would leave it for him and would not ask him [for it] neither at the first palace, nor at the second, nor at the third, nor at the fourth, nor at the fifth, nor at the sixth, nor at the seventh palace. He would only show them his seals and they would leave him alone and he would enter.

3. At the gate to the sixth palace, Dumiel the prince, guardian of the threshold of the right of the sixth palace, sits on a bench of pure *yetok* in which is the radiance of the lights of heaven as at the Creation of the world. Adastan Iran Adastan Kafino Shamnush Akhshene-YHVH, Lord of Israel, and Dumiel, the prince receive him [i.e., the initiate] with a kindly manner and set him on a bench of pure *yetok* and sit next to him on his right.

4. He says to him: I warn and testify before you concerning two things: No one [successfully] goes down to the Merkabah who does not have the following two virtues. He must have repeatedly studied the Torah, the Prophets, and the Holy Writings, and he must have repeatedly studied Mishna, Halacha, Aggada, and the rendering of legal decisions on what is permissible and forbidden. Also, he must have observed all of the Torah in its entirety, observing all the warnings, the statutes, the judgments, and the teachings which were given to Moses on Sinai.

MISHNA 2: We do not know what the gift was.

MISHNA 3: This, according to Smith ("Observations on *Hekhalot Rabbati,*" p. 149) starts the alternate account of the happenings at the gate of the sixth palace. Note the very rabbinic requirements listed in the next mishna.

CHAPTER 22

1. And if one says "I have these two virtues," immediately Dumiel, the prince, becomes attached to him. Gabriel, the scribe, writes on the parchment of the carriage of that man, saying, "Such is the knowledge of this particular person and such are his deeds and he requests to enter before the Throne of Glory."

2. As soon as the guards of the gate of the seventh palace see him, with Dumiel and Gabriel and Katspiel proceeding in front of the carriage of that man who is worthy and descends to the Merkabah, their faces, which were wrathful, are paled, they loosen their taut bows and return their sharp swords to the sheaths. Nevertheless, one must show them the great seal and the awesome crown of Ayir, Suber, Metzugeyah, and Beshpitash-YHVH, Lord of Israel. They then conduct him before the Throne of Glory. They bring before him all types of music and song, and they make music and a parade before him until they raise him and seat him near the Cherubim, near the Wheels, and near the Holy Hayot. He sees wonders and powers, majesty and greatness, holiness and purity, terror and meekness and righteousness, at the same time.

3. Rabbi Ishmael said: All the *haverim* [i.e., the initiated] liken this to a man who has a ladder in the middle of his house, who ascends and descends on it and there is no creature who stops him. Blessed are you, Lord, God Who knows all secrets and is the Lord of hidden things. Amen. Amen.

MISHNA 2: The narrative of the ascent is resumed here and continues to 24:3. The initiate has passed the test of the sixth palace, and now the terrifying guards of the seventh palace (cf. 17:8–18:2) let him pass unharmed. Note the full Ezekelian panoply of heavenly beings.

MISHNA 3: The ladder theme has occurred before in 15:2. The blessing is very rabbinic in style and occurs again in 25:4 and 28:2.

4. R. Ishmael said: R. Shimon b. Gamliel became angry with me and said: There was almost destruction in our vineyard. This [refers] to Patria-YHVH, Lord of Israel. Why did you unknowingly err with us? Did you believe that Yonathan b. Uziel was an insignificant man in Israel? What if he came and simply stood before the gate of the seventh palace?

5. R. Ishmael said: I immediately went and was angry with R. Nehunya b. Hakkanah and said: Oh, prince of anger, why do I yet live? And he said to me: Son of the Proud Ones, if it [has come to] this, what [good] is my presence among you? I have put into your mouths the Torah, the Prophets, and the Holy Writings; the Mishna, the midrash of laws and legends, the legal decisions of the permissible and the forbidden. Yet were it not for the secrets of Torah which I have hidden from you, would you have come and appeared before me at all? I know why you have come. You only came to hear about the guards of the seventh palace.

MISHNA 4: This section (22:4–23:5) picks up the fact that in 17:8 R. Nehunya did not specify the *names* of the guards of the gate of the seventh palace although he did describe them as fierce. Not knowing these names could be very dangerous, for one would not be able to counter their power. R. Shimon ben Gamliel is the *Nasi,* the patriarch of the Jews recognized by Rome and the head of the community and the court. He notes the absence of the names and indicates that even the very pious Yonathan b. Uziel would be subjected to danger without the names. R. Nehunya, as the next mishna indicates, is reluctant to divulge the names. His conversation with R. Ishmael seems to take place during the trance.

CHAPTER 23

1. Go tell the *Nasi:* Concerning all of the guards of the gates of the six palaces one has authority to make mention of the names of God and to use them [magically], but as for the guards of the gates of the seventh palace, the very hearing of these names causes a man to be thrown into a panic as to how to use them, because the name of each and every one of them is derived from the name of the King of the Universe and I have not specified them. Now that you say to me "Specify," come stand on your feet, every one of you. When the name of each [guard] comes forth from my mouth, bow down and fall on your faces. Immediately, all the mighty men of the *havura* came and all the mighty of the *yeshiva* stood on their feet before R. Nehunya ben Hakkanah. They would fall while the scribes would write [whenever a name was mentioned].

MISHNA 1: A rabbinic Jew bows down to the ground only on the New Year and the Day of Atonement. The origin of this custom is the report that on the Day of Atonement, in Temple times, the high priest would enter the Holy of Holies to atone for the sins of the people. In the course of the sacrificial service, the high priest confessed three times, and as part of each confession, he would recite a verse from the Bible with the Tetragrammaton in it. At that point, and only at that point, was the Tetragrammaton pronounced properly, i.e., according to the ancient Tradition. At all other times, according to the rabbis, some substitute was used so as not to use the real pronunciation in a profane setting. When the Tetragrammaton was pronounced on the Day of Atonement in the Temple, the people who heard it fell on their faces in prostration and reverence. It may be this which occurs here as R. Nehunya mentions the names of the guards of the gate of the seventh palace.

2. These are the names of the guards of the gate of the seventh palace specified by the ascent: [1] Ḥorpaniel Zehaftria-YHVH, Lord of Israel—a revered, esteemed, and awesome prince; [2] Avirzahia Kavpiel-YHVH, Lord of Israel—a revered, esteemed, and awesome prince; [3] Atargiel-YHVH, Lord of Israel; [4] Hatrogiel Bangiel-YHVH, Lord of Israel Hash—a revered, esteemed, and awesome prince, terrifying, noble, glorified, powerful, and mighty; [5] Sastetiel-YHVH, Lord of Israel—a revered, esteemed, and awesome prince, terrifying, noble, glorified, powerful, mighty, and valiant; [6] Anaphiel-YHVH, Lord of Israel—a revered, awesome, terrifying, noble, glorified, powerful, mighty, and valiant prince whose name is mentioned before the Throne of Glory three times every day, in the heavens, from the day the world was created until now, in praise, because the signet ring of the heavens and of the earth is given into his power.

3. And as soon as everyone in heaven would see him [i.e., Anaphiel], they would fall on their faces and prostrate themselves before him. This, however, was not usually done in heaven. For if you reason that they [all the angels] bow only to the Angel of the Presence [and not to Anaphiel, this is not the case. Rather] only those who stand outside [the presence] of the Throne of Glory bow down [to the Angel of the Presence while those who do stand in its presence] do not bow down to the Angel of the Presence. But [even] they [i.e., those in the Throne-room] bow down to Anaphiel, the prince, willingly and with the permission of Atratas, the great master, Aphimiel Shama Birtsa-YHVH, Lord of Israel.

4. These are the names of the guards of the gate of the seventh palace specified by the descent. Those which were separated were the names of Tofiel and Liviel. [1] Trapiel-YHVH—an exalted, commanding,

---

MISHNA 2: There is one set of guards for going in and one set for going out. Or, if ascent and descent indicate different mystical techniques, each technique has its own guards. Note that the names are more complex than the others, and that this is the "YHVH, Lord of Israel" family but that there appear to be only six guards (and not eight). Anaphiel clearly outranks them all.

MISHNA 3: The "YHVH" family appears to outrank the "Presence" family, for those inside the Throne-room bow down to the former and not to the latter.

MISHNA 4: Again, only six names. Again, all YHVH names. I do not know what "separated" means here. Is it meant to round out one of these numbers to eight?

awesome prince named Abirazhaya-YHVH; [2] Dalkukiel-YHVH—an exalted, commanding, awesome prince named Livavpiel-YHVH; [3] Yikriel-YHVH—an exalted, commanding, awesome prince named Atargiel-YHVH; [4] Yasheshiel-YHVH—an exalted, commanding, awesome prince named Binana-YHVH; [5] Trafiel-YHVH—an exalted, commanding, awesome prince named Zohaliel-YHVH; [6] Anaphiel-YHVH—an exalted, commanding, awesome prince named Shofsiel-YHVH, strong, righteous, and valiant.

5. Why is his name Anaphiel? It is because of the branch of the crown of crowns that rests on his head, covering and veiling all the chambers of the palace of Aravot-Rakia. He is like the Creator of the World for, just as it is written about the Creator of the World, "his glory covered the heavens" [Habakkuk 3:3], so Anaphiel is the attendant prince who is cited by the name of his master. Why, then, is he the most beloved of all the guards of the gates of the six palaces? It is because he opens the gates of the seventh palace. There are two hundred and ninety-six faces of the Holy Hayot opposite the gate of the seventh palace.

MISHNA 5: Anaphiel means "the branch of God." The analogy is with the figure of the Yotser Bereshit, which, as Scholem has pointed out, is a demiurge—i.e., a very highly placed heavenly figure who actually does the work of forming and creating (cf. Sefer Yetsira and the conclusion to this unit). The analogy seems to be that both are very highly placed servants, both have divine elements in their names (*Yotser*—creator, *'El*—God), and both shield reality from the intensity of the divine Presence. Not even the highest of the angels can stand before His total Presence. Therefore, Anaphiel must shield them from God.

Several manuscripts read 296 and several read 256. The latter may be correct as follows: There are four Hayot (cf. Ezekiel 1). Each has four faces, here taken as four heads. Each head has four faces. Each face has four profiles (two sides, front and rear). This yields $4 \times 4 \times 4 \times 4 = 256$.

CHAPTER 24

1. The greatest [terror] of them all is the five hundred and twelve eyes of the four Holy Hayot opposite the gate of the seventh palace. [There are also] faces of human shape—and each "face" has sixteen faces—on each Hayah opposite the gate of the seventh palace.

2. As soon as that man [i.e., the initiate] entreats to descend to the Merkabah, Anaphiel the prince, opens the doors of the seventh palace and that man enters and stands on the threshold of the gate of the seventh palace and the Holy Hayot lift him up. Five hundred and twelve eyes, and each and every eye of the eyes of the Holy Hayot is hollow like the holes in a sieve woven of branches. These eyes appear like lightning, and they dart to and fro. In addition, there are the eyes of the Cherubim of Might and the Wheels of the Shekhina, which are similar to torches of light and the flames of burning coals.

3. This man then trembles, shakes, moves to and fro, panics, is terrified, faints, and collapses backwards. Anaphiel, the prince, and sixty-three watchmen of the seven gates of the palace support him, and they all help him and say: "Do not fear, son of the beloved seed. Enter and see the King in His magnificence. You will not be slaughtered and you will not be burnt."

MISHNA 1: Imagine: the gates to the seventh palace open, and you see the four Ezekelian Hayot, all of towering proportions. There are 256 faces and, hence, 512 eyes staring at you. Note the vivid description of the eyes. Remember that Ezekiel's Wheels are intelligent, i.e., have eyes.

MISHNA 3: The mystic is overwhelmed by fear as well as by awe. Such is the nature of the truly spiritual. He is saved, however, by the merit of his chosen-people ancestry.

4. Illustrious King, glorious King, masterful King, blessed King, chosen King, luminescent King, distinguished King, heroic King, sublime King, omniscient King, remarkable King, disciplining King, splendiferous King, majestic King, affluent King, eternal King, aristocratic King, infinite King, memorable King, worthy King, radiating King, living King, merciful King, pious King, valuable King, chaste King, righteous King, esteemed King, redeeming King, astounding King, adorned King, worshipped King, sympathetic King, commanding King, fervent King, comprehending King, possessing King, prosperous King, gilded King, faithful King, resplendent King, secretive King, wise King, modest King, benevolent King, patient King, embellished King, rescuing King, virtuous King, joyous King, radiant King, sanctified King, esoteric King, commended King, revered King, compassionate King, moderate King, attentive King, tranquil King, serene King, ornamented King, perfect King, supportive King. Blessed be He.

5. They give him strength. Immediately, they blow a trumpet from "above the vault which is over the heads of the Hayot" [Ezekiel 1:25]. And the Holy Hayot cover their faces and the Cherubim and the Wheels turn their faces away and he stands erect, turns, and poses himself before the Throne of Glory.

MISHNA 4: This is one of the many hymns that follow. It is an acrostic (which cannot be captured in the English) and has a hypnotic rhythm (which also eludes translation). Scholem has called the effect one of a giant flywheel. Perhaps this (and the other hymns) have some musical analogy in Bach's rendering of the doxology of Isaiah 6.

MISHNA 5: To be actually before the Throne of God Himself!

CHAPTER 25

1. As soon as he stands before the Throne of Glory, he begins to chant the hymn that the Throne of Glory recites every day: a prayer, laud, song, blessing, praise, extolment, exultation, appreciation, acknowledgment, victory, melody, meditation, homage, joyfulness, celebration, rejoicing, worship, gracefulness, modesty, luster, magnification, faithfulness, righteousness; virtuous, treasured, decorated, valorous, jubilant, elated, superior, contented, restful, consoled, tranquil, serene, peaceful, benevolent, invincible, valued, compelling, compassionate, graceful, magnanimous, elegant, embellished, adored, revered, merciful, luminescent, resplendent, privileged, brilliant, phenomenal, crowned, glittering, far-reaching, distressed, miraculous, liberating, redolent, illuminating, royal, remedying, daring, dynamic, grandiose, precious, powerful, commanding, valiant, pleasurable, majestic, splendorous, courageous, heroic, sanctified, chaste, pure, proud, eminent, magnificent, royally dignified; honor and splendor to Harariel-YHVH, Lord of Israel, a King Who is adorned and ornamented with embroidery of hymns, the One Who is beautified in splendor, esteemed in glory, reverence, and beauty, abundant in majesty, an awesome crown Whose Name is sweet to Him and whose memory is pleasing, and a beautiful crown. To Him they give thanks. He is exquisite, and His palace glorifies Him. His attendants sing pleasingly to Him, and the righteous [sing pleasingly] of His power and wonders:

King of the king of kings, God of Gods, and Lord of Lords,
Who is surrounded with chains of crowns,
Who is encompassed by the cluster of the rulers of radiance,
Who covers the heavens with the wing of His magnificence,
    And in His majesty appeared from the heights,
    From His beauty the deeps are kindled,
    And from His stature the heavens are sparked.
His stature sends out the lofty,

MISHNA 1: These celestial hymns must be appreciated as best as is possible in translation. Note the terms which form the "universe of religious (spiritual) discourse," the language of religion. What do these words mean to you?

80

And His crown blazes out the mighty,
And His garment flows with the precious.
And all trees shall rejoice in His word,
And herbs shall exult in His rejoicing,
And His words shall drop as perfumes,
Flowing forth in flames of fire,
Giving joy to those who search them,
And quiet to those who fulfill them.

2. A king beloved and adored by them, faultless and proud. One who takes pride in the Proud Ones and strengthens all mortals. He glorifies kings, praises youths, and makes modest the arrogant. He is a joy in the mouth of all who call Him, sweet to all who wait expectantly for Him, superb in all His ways, upright in all His deeds, lucid in counsel and knowledge, clear in understanding, and unequivocal in judgment of all flesh. He is a witness in all cases. He is the judge of everything. Mighty in knowledge and in every mystery, and glorious in sanctity and purity.

3. A true and solitary King, a King perfect in His deeds and one Who nourishes His creations, an enduring King, a King Who brings death and life, a King Who creates every blessing and establishes all good. A blessed King, a King Who is unique, exalted, mighty. A distinguished helper, patient, holy, pure, righteous, true, upright, faithful, and vigorous. A King Who is outstanding in that He loosens the knots of exaltation and is set above the pillars of sublimity, the chambers of the palace. He watches secret places and understands profundities. He beholds the dark places wherever He is and He does not renege on His own words and desire. He does not change location to flee from him [man] and does not hide to conceal Himself from his [man's] presence.

4. You will rule forever—merciful, gracious, forgiving, lenient King Who causes [time] to go on and pass away. You will be revered in every hymn, exalted on Your Throne of Glory. Treasured is Your every grace, lauded in every exultation, praised in every magnification, applauded in every prayer, glorified forever, sanctified forever unto Tootrusea-YHVH, Lord of Israel. Lord, King of existence, master of

---

MISHNA 2: What is the mood of this hymn? Is it different from that of the previous one?

MISHNA 4: Here, Tootruseah-YHVH seems to be God Himself or, at least, the being perceived on the Throne. What is so strange about that? Why are these properly call hymns, and not poems?

all deeds, wise in all secrets, ruler in all generations, sole God Who since eternity has been King alone, Who is forever and ever. Selah. Who is like unto you Tootrusea-YHVH, Lord of Israel, master of the mighty? To you, Tootrusea-YHVH, Lord of Israel; they praise the Throne of Your Glory. To you they give majesty and much strength and adornment. For you they are courageous, for you they are heroic, for you they are joyous. They sing to you, they meditate on you. They bless you, they flatter you, they exalt you, they adorn you, they uplift you, they glorify you, they make you majestic, they revere you, they worship you, they sanctify you, Tootrusea-YHVH, Lord of Israel. Your attendants will crown You with a diadem and sing a new hymn to You. You will rule forever and be called One forever, because You are God, Lord of Israel, mighty, abundantly redeeming, a God wise in Your rule and wise in Your realm. Blessed are you, Lord, God of Israel, wise in secrets and Lord of hidden things. Amen. Amen.

CHAPTER 26

1. I saw one "like the lightning" [Ezekiel 1:27] who examines if one is worthy to descend to the Merkabah or not. If one is worthy to descend to the Merkabah, when they say to him "Enter," he does not enter. They repeat it to him, "Enter," and he enters immediately. They praise him as though to say, certainly this is one of the descenders of the Merkabah. But if he is not worthy to descend to the Merkabah, when they say to him "Enter," he enters immediately. They then throw thousands of iron bars on him.

2. The guards of the gates of the sixth palace make a mirage for him of a million waves of water and there is not any water there, not even a drop. And if one says: "What is the nature of this water?" they immediately run after him, stoning him and say: "Numbskull, perhaps you are from the seed of those who kissed the Golden Calf; you are not worthy to see the King and His Throne of Glory." He does not move from there until they throw a million bars of iron on him.

3. You perform valorous deeds and make new works. He renews His creatures every day. He causes His attendants to be excited and shine in the midst of the myriads. You reject hatred, jealousy, hostility, and rivalry. You are slow to anger, You annul the quarrelsome wrath of all living things. The best of the Cherubim of Your Glory are made of fire but He is above the Cherubim of fire, above the blazing Seraphim, surrounding Your Throne of Glory, standing one next to another. They announce: "Clear a pathway for Him Who rides above the universe" [Psalms 68:5]. Much blessing and praise and homage, hymn, appreciation, acknowledgement, adornment, charm, humility, lovingkindness, strengthening, making bold, making lordly, separating, choosing, testing, making heroic, making proud, making exalted. In their mouths are hymns and songs, on their tongues are rejoicings. They do not slumber, not at night or during the day, but are like a light that shines forth song and praise.

MISHNA 1: This, together with the next mishna, is a flashback to the dangers of the gates of the sixth palace. Mishna 3 picks up the hymns again.

4. You are a king who is great, heroic, awesome, blessed, valiant, prominent, splendid, distinguished, meritorious, active, chaste, worthy, tremendous, fascinating, destructive, captivating, mysterious, patient, redeeming, joyous, sanctified, merciful, concerned, supportive, forbearing, magnanimous, and faithful.

5. You are Lord, God of Gods, Lord of Lords. You are great—all the great aggrandize You. You are mighty—all the mighty declare You great. You are awesome—all the awesome fear You. You are righteous—all the righteous declare You upright. You are pious—all the pious long for You. You are sanctified—all the sanctified consecrate You. You are faithful—all the faithful believe in You.

CHAPTER 27

1. You are the One Who revealed the secret to Moses and did not conceal from him all Your heroic deeds. When the words were departing from Your mouth, the heavens trembled and stood in panic [before You]. All were burnt in the blazes of fire. You test the kidneys and the hearts [emotions and intellect], and prefer the trustworthy. You dwell in the flame, an image in the flame of fire, forming as does the flame of a fire. You are mighty and proud above all the boastful, and exalted above all. You humiliate the arrogant and raise up the humble. Blessed be He.

2. The most proud among the creatures in man. The likeness of man have You set into Your Throne of Glory: They [the Cherubim] have the face of a man and a man's hand is under their wings. They run like a man, labor like a man, sow, and bow in prayers [like a man]. And awe of You is king over them.

3. The most proud among the domesticated animals is the ox. The likeness of an ox have You set into Your Throne of Glory: They [the Cherubim] have the face of an ox. They run like an ox, they work like an ox, and they stand in their place like an ox. And awe of You is holy over them.

4. The most proud among the wild animals is the lion. The likeness of a lion have You set in Your Throne of Glory: They [the Cherubim] have the face of a lion. Their roar is like a lion's, the fear [the cast] is like a lion's, and the power of their arm is like a lion's. And awe of You is powerful over them.

5. The most proud among the birds is the eagle. The likeness of an eagle have You set into Your Throne of Glory: They [the Cherubim] have the face of an eagle. Their speed is like an eagle's, their wrath is like an eagle's, and their flight is like an eagle's. And awe of You is pure over them. All these declare Your holiness three times [daily] with the threefold sanctification as it is said: "Holy Holy Holy is God, the Lord of Hosts, the whole world is full of His Glory" [Isaiah 6:3].

MISHNA 1: This is based on Ezekiel 1.

CHAPTER 28

1. Excellence and faithfulness—are His Who lives forever
   Understanding and blessing—are His Who lives forever
   Grandeur and greatness—are His Who lives forever
   Cognition and expression—are His Who lives forever
   Magnificence and majesty—are His Who lives forever
   Counsel and strength—are His Who lives forever
   Luster and brilliance—are His Who lives forever
   Grace and benevolence—are His Who lives forever
   Purity and goodness—are His Who lives forever
   Unity and honor—are His Who lives forever
   Crown and glory—are His Who lives forever
   Precept and practice—are His Who lives forever
   Sovereignty and rule—are His Who lives forever
   Adornment and permanence—are His Who lives forever
   Mystery and wisdom—are His Who lives forever
   Might and meekness—are His Who lives forever
   Splendor and wonder—are His Who lives forever
   Righteousness and honor—are His Who lives forever
   Invocation and holiness—are His Who lives forever
   Exultation and nobility—are His Who lives forever
   Song and hymn—are His Who lives forever
   Praise and glory—are His Who lives forever

MISHNA 1: This hymn is still part of certain rabbinic liturgies. It, too, is an acrostic and it rhymes.

2. Who can relate one of the billion, one of the myriad of myriads of Your mighty deeds. O King of the kings of kings, Blessed be He. For the Holy Hayot are present and stand erect before you. They are the "still small voice" [I Kings 19:12]. Fire is their way, the fire of furnaces, and they are in awe of the fire, lest they be burned in the blazing fire. They surround You, they encircle You; near them, hidden in Your midst, they meditate on the secret and the profound. They are girded with might; they are enveloped in grandeur. The eye does not gaze upon Your sword, because You are a sanctified King, ruler of the ones above and the ones below, of the ancestors and the descendants. There is no one among the ones above and the ones below, no one of the ancestors and of the descendants who is able to understand Your actions and examine Your mighty deeds. How many there are who cannot see Aleph, Bet, and Gimel, and none of them [can see] Metatron, whose name is cited by eight names: Margiyiel is his name. Geyotiel is his name. Zeyotiel is his name. Achahiel is his name. Keyoiel is his name. Yehoiel Oziheyah Ozehoiel Sagnesgiel Sagdiel is his name. Sagnasyeriah Sagnesgiel Sagnesoilah is his name. And because of the love with which they love him in heaven, he is called: Metatron, the servant of God in the Holy Army, forbearing and renowned for benevolence. Blessed are You, God, wise in secrets and Lord of hidden things. Amen. Amen. Selah. Selah.

3. Rabbi Ishmael said: Thus said Rabbi Akiva in the name of Rabbi Eliezer, the great: From the day that the Torah was given until the Second Temple was built, the Torah had been given but her splendor, her dignity, her greatness, her honor, her magnificence, her fear, her terror, her awe, her riches, her majesty, her excellence, her might, her glory, and her reverence had not been given forth until the Second Temple was built. [But] the Shekhina [Divine Presence] did not dwell in it. [Variant: for the Shekhina (Divine Presence) did dwell in it.]

MISHNA 3: Something is wrong here.

CHAPTER 29

1. Israel was ready to vent grievances before its Father Who is in heaven, to say: Many misfortunes are befalling us—a great hardship and a huge burden. You said to us, Build Me a house and even though you build, occupy yourself with Torah. This is His response to His servants:

2. Although a great idleness was upon you from the Exile, I longed for the time when I would hear the words of Torah from your mouths. I was angry with you because you did not act correctly, you opposed My majesty. And I rose and I utterly destoyed the cities and houses and the students attending conferences. I did not act correctly when I rose to oppose you and when I commanded a decree upon you. Undoubtedly, it will persist forever and be to Me a source of vexation which will not last only for one, two, ten, or thirty years—or even, with strength, for one hundred or more. Yet, you persuaded Me that you would behave correctly, and I accepted upon Myself your reprimand.

3. Because the laments of Israel are sweet to Me and cover Me with desire, your words plead in My ears and the speech of your mouths is acceptable to Me. Occupy yourselves with the house of My choice and let not the Torah be removed from your mouths. I am the Master of marvels, I am the Lord of separateness [perishut]. I am the Lord of wonders and miracles. I am called "the Lord of valor." Before Me, miracles happen, and [everyone] before My Throne of Glory is astounded. Who has come before Me to whom I have not given peace? Who has called to Me whom I have not answered? [Who has not] made his requests of Me?

MISHNA 1: Here the text turns to a more usual theological vein: the problem of the suffering of the Jewish people. Having seen God (His Throne, to be exact) and having praised Him, the rabbi-mystic now poses the problem. God begins His answer, which does not seem to be very clear and is of no direct concern to us here, interesting though it is.

4. I have My depositories and My treasuries, and there is nothing missing in them. Make your requests, [state] the desires of your souls, immediately it shall be done because there is no season like this season, for My soul tarries until I see you. And there is no time like this time when your love is bound up in My breast.

5. I know what you desire, and My heart recognizes what you crave. You desire more Torah, multitudes [of students], and a larger portion of traditions. You wait expectantly to discuss the Law. You desire fiercely the multitude of My secrets. [You desire deeply] to expand the Torah, to do wonders of strength as mountains upon mountains, to make the Torah wondrous in the streets, and to multiply discussion on the avenues, to make the Torah as great as the sands of the sea and My secrets as the dust of the earth . . .

MISHNA 5: The continuation of this text deals with theodicy. It is no longer properly mystical.

Conclusion

Our study of *Ma'aseh Merkabah,* "The Mechanics of the Vision," as represented by the Pirkei Heikhalot has revealed to us a very strange world. It is a world of strange beings with strange powers. It is a world of mystery and complexity. And it is a world of danger, sublime beauty, and awesomeness.

By whom and for whom was this text written? Like Sefer Yetsira, the Pirkei Heikhalot was written by well-educated orthodox rabbis for other well-educated orthodox rabbis. The names of the sages mentioned in the text, their use of rabbinic law to draw R. Nehunya ben Hakkanah out of his trance, and so on, indicate a decidedly rabbinic context. As to its use, this book was probably the text from which one learned the names of the angel-guards, the magic seals, and the kinds of situations one could anticipate encountering in the ascent.

What do we learn about the heavenly hosts? We learn that they all have names (most of which contain a divine element), that they all have assigned places and tasks in the supernal hierarchy (some being more powerful than others, i.e., closer to the Throne), and that they all have power (power to guard, power to destroy). Hence the mystic needs power, and his power stems from the seals which contain the names of the highest orders of angels, those who "outrank" the angel-guards. Therefore, the name-seals work.

The mystical experience itself (as reported in the text) presupposes moral purity, rabbinic learnedness, ritual purity, and thorough mastery of the special knowledge necessary to negotiate the supernal realm. In the end, the mystic reports three things: that he faints but is supported, that he hears the hymns chanted before the Throne, and that he hears a message from God. He does not tell us what the Throne looks like nor does he report what (if anything) sits on the Throne. Rather, he specifically states that the Ultimate is veiled by the wings of Anaphiel. The hymns he records are certainly hypnotic, generating a momentum of their own (which cannot really be caught in translation).

What type of mystical experience is it? It is *not* a unification of the mystic with God. It is not even a separation of the soul from the body, or a return of the separated soul to its Source. It *is* an ecstasy, not in the proper sense of the word ("standing outside oneself") but in the general, sublime sense of the word. It is not a descent into one's own self or a voyage into nothingness, but a coming-before the King. Properly put, this type of mysticism is a "visionary mysticism"—"visionary" because the mystic sees and hears something of the supernal world, and "mystical" because he must prepare for it and work toward it. One other very significant note: This is a form of group mysticism. The rabbi takes his amanuensis, his pupils, and his colleagues with him. He can do it alone, in his house, but it is also usable in small groups.

Having studied these two texts, we are ready to deal with the general questions about the audience, context, use, and ambiance of this type of literature. We turn to that now.

6
GENERAL CONCLUSION

Now that the drama of the *Ma'aseh Bereshit* and the *Ma'aseh Merkabah* has, in part, been unfolded before us, we must turn to the task of reflecting upon this material, and several general questions must be answered.

Who is the readership for such materials as we have encountered in Sefer Yetsira and Pirkei Heikhalot? As stated before, the authors, editors, readers, and practitioners of this material were all well-educated orthodox rabbis. As such, this material is as much a part of rabbinic literature as its more well known counterparts: the Talmud, the Midrash, and the Liturgy. Yet not every orthodox rabbi was either fit or willing to be exposed to this material. It is, thus, intended for an esoteric elite within the scholarly community of rabbis. Actually, this is strange, for in other cultures, the primal powers of the universe can be touched by the nonscholarly. The "mana" is not usually confined to an esoteric elite of a scholarly class. Yet it was so in Rabbinic Judaism.

What are the contexts of this material? As indicated, the contexts of Sefer Yetsira and Pirkei Heikhalot are two: the Biblical, for both are an extension of their respective Biblical "sources," and the Hellenistic. Such elements as the Greek words which serve as names of God, the alphabetology and numerology, the mass of beings arranged in a hierarchy, and so on, are evidence of this. There are also parallels from early Christianity and the Dead Sea Scrolls; the interested student must follow this further. And, again as indicated, all these "influences" are subsumed under the theology of Rabbinic Judaism.

What are the main characteristics of this material? First, there is the magical element. We have seen this in the letters and the sealed dimensions of Creation, in the instructions for man-made creation, in the name-seals of the ascent, and even in the very structure of the names of the angels and in the formulaic pattern of the hymns. Also, because it is a magical world, it is a mechanical world, a world of forces seeking balance. Second, this is a system torn between secrecy and explicitness, between the need to conceal and the need to reveal. Thus, the secrets are revealed, but only reluctantly and then only in part. Thus, too, the imagery is shockingly anthropomorphic and concrete, yet the Ultimate is veiled. One aspect of this dialectic is the pseudepigraphy: Sefer Yetsira is ascribed to Abraham, and Pirkei Heikhalot to R. Nehunya ben Hakkanah, thus attempting to generate layers within layers of authoritative tradition which justify revealing the secrets. Third, this is a very dynamic system. There is a lot of movement—of letters, of angels, of hymns. There is a lot of hustle and bustle on high. Fourth, we learn from this literature that Merkabah mysticism was both a body of knowledge and a Way, a "gnosis" and a "praxis"; that, as the following story indicates, this knowledge was not a body of abstract ideas held together only by the mind. Rather, it was a knowledge that was intimately intertwined with concrete mystical activity.

Once Rabban Yohanan ben Zakkai was riding on an ass, when going on a journey. Rabbi Eleazar ben Arakh was driving the ass from behind.

Rabbi Eleazar said to him, "Master, teach me a chapter of the work of the chariot."

He answered him, "Have I not taught you thus, *Nor may the work of the chariot be taught in the presence of one, unless he is a sage and understands of his own knowledge?*"

Rabbi Eleazar then said to him. "Master, permit me to say before you something which you have taught me."

He answered, "Say on!"

Forthwith, Rabban Yohanan ben Zakkai dismounted from the ass, wrapped himself up in his cloak, and sat upon a stone beneath an olive tree.

Said Rabbi Eleazar to him, "Master, why did you dismount from the ass?"

He answered, "Is it proper that I should ride upon an ass while you are expounding the work of the chariot, and the Divine Presence is with us, and the ministering angels accompany us?"

Forthwith Rabbi Eleazar ben Arakh began his exposition of the work of the chariot. Fire came down from heaven and encompassed all the trees of the field. All the trees began to utter song.

And what was the song they uttered? *Praise the Lord from the earth, you sea monsters and all depths, fire and hail, snow and frost, stormy wind fulfilling his command, mountains and all hills, fruit trees and all cedars* (Ps. 148:79).

An angel then answered from the fire and said, "This is the very work of the chariot."

Thereupon Rabban Yohanan ben Zakkai rose and kissed him on his head and said, "Blessed be the Lord, God of Israel, who has given a son to Abraham our father who knows to speculate upon and to investigate and to expound the work of the chariot. There are some who preach well but do not perform well. Others perform well but do not expound well! But you expound well and perform well. Happy are you, O Abraham our father, that Rabbi Eleazar ben Arakh has come forth from your loins.''*

Ma'aseh Merkabah was practiced as well as preached. This body of knowledge was accessible to man through tradition, reflection, *and* experience.

Of what did this body of knowledge consist? It consisted, in the first instance, of a view as to the nature of reality. In this view, reality forms one continuum from the inert stone to the divine Throne. There is no sharp division between nature and supernature. Rather, reality is an order of beings which includes the physical world, man, the celestial worlds, and the supra-celestial realms of the angels and the other heavenly beings. This entire range of beings is, however, secondary with respect to the utterly transcendent, the numinous reality which is beyond even mystical visions. Furthermore, reality, as it is known to the mystic, is created (or generated). And throughout, even in its uppermost reaches, reality is motivated by spirit, by the word, by the name. Word, name, and number form the real substructure of the world. Names, and even sounds, are the true keys to the gates to the infinite. Supernal, like mundane, reality is fraught with danger, and both are shaped by the power and the order of the spirit.

The body of knowledge of the Merkabah mystic, therefore, comprised a cosmological theory rooted in the spirit plus a practicable knowledge of the paths into that realm. The mystic needed to understand how reality was formed of names, words, letters, sounds, and numbers. He needed to know the sequence of the heavenly palaces, with their guards. And he needed to know what was expected of him and what was forbidden to him in this world and in that one.

The mystic, then, took this body of knowledge, this "gnosis," and used it, making it into a "praxis." With it he could often perform what appeared to the common man as miracles. He could "create." And with it he could transcend his earthly bounds and enter the realm of the spirit. It was not ethics, law, theology, or preaching that the Merkabah mystic generated. It was reports of the heavenly realms and the creative acts of man.

What is the implied theology of this literature? God is absolutely transcendent. Monotheism is supreme. No magic compels God. No angel outranks God. He is not even perceived; only His minions and His Throne can be seen, through the veils. Also, God does not reach out to man. Man approaches Him. Man, when properly prepared, can approach God at will. He can ascend the ladder or take up the letters. But it is man who initiates here, not God.

---

*Cited from J. Neusner, *First Century Judaism in Crisis* (New York and Nashville: Abingdon Press, 1975), pp. 127-28.

What motivated this literature? What sensitivities, feelings, and human interests generated this strange world? The texts as we have them are not motivated by an intimacy with God. On the contrary, man and God are far apart. Neither the creative act nor the mystical act is a moment of love or devotion. Why, then, did these rabbi-mystics and rabbi-magicians occupy themselves with this complex material? There are several reasons. First, there is a certain curiosity, a search for knowledge, that leads people to explore the hidden. Second, the Biblical texts did require explication and expansion, and in the context of a general salvific theology based on study and practice, mystical knowledge and activity were seen as an integral part of the divine plan of Redemption. To get to know God and His ways—esoteric as well as exoteric—was to come a step closer to personal, national, and cosmic salvation. But third, and most important, these texts reflect man's preoccupation with the holy. It is the numinous itself which attracts people's minds and efforts. It is the mysterious powerfulness of the realm of the Other that rivets man's attention upon such phenomena and such texts. These esotericist rabbis comprehended the numinous in the framework of their time, but the wrestling with it is as old as man's spiritual sensitivity and insight. To study and practice Sefer Yetsira or Pirkei Heikhalot was to deal with the numinous, and that was reason enough.

If I were to characterize this mysticism, in its creative and its visionary forms, with one word, I would call it "power mysticism." This is because the core of these bodies of knowledge, experiences, and activities is a moment of power—power to create, power and counterpower during the ascent, and, ultimately, the power of God. The vision is a royal vision; the expression, an expression of power.

To the best of my knowledge, these mystical ascents and creative acts are no longer practiced, and these visions are no longer seen by men. What happened? What was the fate of this "power mysticism"? First, the literature was destined to survive. Fragments, some badly mutilated, have been transmitted over the centuries, and they are only now receiving another life from the hands of scholars. Second, certain themes were to find their echoes in later mystical literature. Thus, the Merkabah, with all its accompanying celestial hosts, takes its place in the Zoharic scheme of things, and even in late Hasidic thought it is an integral part of the ontological hierarchy. The Shi'ur Qomah literature, which comes from this period and describes the "body" of God as of colossal dimensions, is fully exploited in certain parts of the Zohar. Third, the use of magical names and seals generated a tradition of "practical Kabbalah" that has lasted until the modern period and still survives in certain sectors of the Jewish community. One need only examine the obverse side of the parchment of most *mezuzot* to find a magical inscription which uses a reverse alphabet. (An excellent study of Jewish magic for the medieval period is J. Trachtenberg,

Jewish Magic and Superstition [1939; reprinted, New York: Atheneum, 1970].)

The most important trace of Merkabah mysticism, however, is to be found in the liturgy of Rabbinic Judaism. Thus, the hymn "Excellence and faithfulness are His Who lives forever" (Pirkei Heikhalot 28:1) is actually a part of the liturgy. Similarly, some of the poems utilized on the High Holidays are of the Heikhalot form and tone, and even the daily liturgy makes use of the multiplicative, hypnotic style of the Heikhalot literature. Also, the occurrence of certain phrases, such as "Creator of creation" (*Yotser Bershit*), and "He is beautiful in glory on the Merkabah" (*ve-nehedar bi-khavod 'al ha-Merkabah*), and "it is not possible to estimate the Merkavot of Your Name, nor to explain Its hiddenness," is evidence of Merkabah influence in the liturgy. More subtly, the angelology of the morning liturgy and the doxology (known as the *Kedusha*) are evidences of an attempt by the liturgists to somehow allude to the mystical experiences of the Merkabah tradition. Similarly, the theme of "parallel doxology" (that the earthly doxology parallels the celestial one) and perhaps even the entire theme of God's kingship—which constitutes one of the central insights of Rabbinic Judaism (see, e.g., M. Kadushin, *The Rabbinic Mind* [New York: Jewish Theological Seminary, 1953])—are indicative of the efforts of the liturgists to come to terms with the insights and experiences of this mystical realm.

It must be added that these Merkabah elements were not simply added to, or incorporated into, the rabbinic liturgy. A close comparison of these two types of texts shows that the rabbi-liturgists acted upon the material in three important ways. They eliminated the ascent and the name-seal themes, and they greatly attenuated the splendor of the celestial personnel and hymns, thereby creating a truly modest and more subtle rendition of the mystical element in worship. They also intertwined the mystical themes with other rabbinic themes, such as the Torah, study, purity of heart, redemption, history, etc. In so doing, the rabbis added a subtle mystical element to Rabbinic Judaism, and they "saved" Merkabah mysticism from becoming a historical curiosity. By "taming" Merkabah mysticism, the rabbis made it part of the living religious tradition of the people.

Certain elements of the Merkabah tradition, however, were destined to die out. The whole world-view of late antiquity, of which it is so much a part, dissipated in the face of the new Islamic-Hellenistic synthesis. More elegant conceptions of the supramundane world were to arise. More sophisticated articulations of the nature of divinity were just under the horizon. And, new and more profound mystical techniques were to appear that were to render the Merkabah tradition inadequate as an expression of the ultimate that man can experience of the divine. It is to one such new synthesis that we now turn.

Unit Two

The Zoharic Tradition

GENERAL INTRODUCTION

The Zohar is a book—a commentary to the Torah, to be exact—written at the end of the thirteenth century in Spain. Yet it is much more than just a book, for within a little more than a century of its publication, the Zohar succeeded in capturing the religious intellect and imagination of vast segments of the educated Jewish community. The Zohar became the "third Bible" of the Jews, second in importance only to the Bible itself and the Talmud. This feat was all the more remarkable because the readership was a sophisticated, educated elite accustomed to dealing with very difficult texts, as we have seen. And yet the Zohar did succeed in carving out a place for itself in the forefront of Jewish thought and practice. We can even say that the Zohar succeeded in creating an entire tradition of its own, an entire stream within the river of the Jewish mystical tradition. How did this happen, and why did it happen? What is the power of the Zohar, and what is the nature of the tradition that is created? How did the Zohar speak to the deepest needs of religious people, acquiring such prominence, so fast, in such sophisticated circles, and generating such profound thought and practice for so many centuries? What were the later developments? How did they modify the teachings of the Zohar? Why? For whom was this literature written, and how was it transmitted? These are the questions of this unit.

The selections presented here are only samples. The sea is vast, and we can walk but a small distance along one shore. Chapter 7 explains how to read the Zohar. Chapter 8 sets forth the teachings of the Zohar on the personality of God. Chapter 9 presents the Zoharic view of the role of man. Chapter 10 traces a later development of these ideas which radicalized them considerably. And Chapter 11 seeks to evaluate the overall impact of this stream of thought.

The ideas contained in this unit are very different from those taught in Sunday school (and certainly from those taught in parochial school). Often they will seem far-out, even heretical, over against the usual received knowledge. In fact, if they do not startle you, you have not fully understood them. Yet these ideas have deep value, for they will teach you something about, and deepen your appreciation of, mystical theology and mystical experience.

7
DOCTRINAL SUMMARY

Introduction

There are three problems which must be resolved before one can even approach the text of the Zohar: (1) the problem of the historical setting and literary structure; (2) the problem of the general intellectual structure, that is, the main ideas; and (3) the problem of how to decipher a Zoharic text.

The core of the historical and literary problem is very simple. The Zohar is a forgery—more exactly, it is pseudepigraphy. The questions arise: How do we know this? Why did the author, who wrote it in the thirteenth century, ascribe it to a second-century figure? Why did he use an artificial language? What streams of thought was the author heir to? These questions have been dealt with in great detail by G. Scholem in several of his works, and a short reading which summarizes his conclusions is presented here. For a fuller discussion of the evidence and methods, the reader should consult Scholem's *Major Trends in Jewish Mysticism,* chapter 5.

The remaining two problems are dealt with in "How to Decipher a Zoharic Text" (below, p. 113).

The Historical Setting and Literary Problems

by G. Scholem*

The book of Zohar, the most important literary work of the Kabbalah, lies before us in some measure inaccessible and silent, as befits a work of secret wisdom. Whether because of this, or in spite of it, among the great literary products of our medieval writings, however much clearer and more familiar than the Zohar many of them seem to us, not one has had an even approximately similar influence or a similar success. To have determined the formation and development over a long period of time of the religious convictions of the widest circles in Judaism, and particularly of those most sensitive to religion, and, what is more, to have succeeded in establishing itself for three centuries, from about 1500 to 1800, as a source of doctrine and revelation equal in authority to the Bible and Talmud, and of the same canonical rank—this is a prerogative that can be claimed by no other work of Jewish literature. This radiant power did not, to be sure, emanate at the very beginning from "The Book of Radiance" or, as we usually render the title in English, "The Book of Splendor." Maimonides' "Guide to the Perplexed," in almost every respect the antithesis of the Zohar, influenced its own time directly and openly; from the moment of its appearance it affected people's minds, moving them to enthusiasm or to consternation. Yet, after two centuries of a profound influence, it began to lose its effectiveness more and more, until finally, for centuries long, it vanished almost entirely from the consciousness of the broad masses. It was only at the end of the 18th century that the Jewish Enlightenment again brought it into prominence, seeking to make it an active force in its own struggle.

From G. Scholem, *Zohar: The Book of Splendor,* rev. ed. (New York: Schocken Books, 1972), pp. 7–21.

It was different with the Zohar, which had to make its way out of an almost complete, hardly penetrable anonymity and concealment. For a hundred years and more it elicited scarcely any interest to speak of. When it came on the scene, it expressed (and therefore appealed to) the feeling of a very small class of men who in loosely organized conventicles strove for a new, mystical understanding of the world of Judaism, and who had not the faintest notion that this particular book alone, among the many which sought to express their new world-view in allegory and symbol, was destined to succeed. Soon, however, the light shadow of scandal that had fallen upon its publication and initial appearance in the world of literature, the enigma of the illegitimate birth of a literary forgery, disappeared and was forgotten. Very slowly but surely the influence of the Zohar grew; and when the groups among which it had gained dominion proved themselves in the storms of Jewish history to be the bearers of a new religious attitude that not only laid claim to, but in fact achieved, authority, then the Zohar in a late but exceedingly intensive afterglow of national life came to fulfil the great historical task of a sacred text supplementing the Bible and Talmud and a new level of religious consciousness. This inspirational character has been attached to it by numerous Jewish groups in Eastern Europe and the Orient down to our own days, nor have they hesitated to assert that final conclusion which has since earliest times been drawn in the recognition of a sacred text, namely, that the effect upon the soul of such a work is in the end not at all dependent upon its being understood.

It was only with the collapse of that stratum of life and belief in which the Kabbalah was able to represent a historical force that the splendor of the Zohar also faded; and later, in the revaluation of the Enlightenment, it became the "book of lies," considered to have obscured the pure light of Judaism. The reform-tending polemic in this case too made haste to become an instrument of historical criticism, which, it must be said, after a few promising starts, showed itself weak and uncertain in the carrying out of its program, sound as its methods and true as many of its theses may have been.

Historical criticism, however, will survive the brief immortality of that "genuine" Judaism whose view of history and whose hierarchy of values gave rise to it. Freed from polemic, and concerned for a more precise and objective insight into its subject matter, it will now assert itself in the new (and in part very old) context in which we begin to see the world of Judaism, and Judaism's history.

LITERARY CHARACTER

The Zohar in its external literary physiognomy seems far from being conceived and constructed as a unified composition. Still less can it be regarded as any kind of systematic exposition of the world-view of the Kabbalah, like many such which have come down to us from the period of the Kabbalah's origin and even more from later times. It is rather, in the printed form that lies before us, a collection of treatises and writings that are considerably different from one another in external form. Most of the sections seem to be interpretations of Bible passages, or short sayings or longer homilies, or else often artfully composed reports of whole series of homilies in which Rabbi Simeon ben Yohai, a famous teacher of the 2nd century, and his friends and students interpret the words of Scripture in accordance with their hidden meaning, and, moreover, almost always in the Aramaic language. Other sections, though these are few, have been preserved in the form of anonymous and purely factual accounts in which there can be recognized no such settings of landscape and persons as those described with so much care elsewhere in the work, often in highly dramatic fashion. Fairly often the exposition is enigmatically brief, but frequently the ideas are very fully presented with homiletical amplitude and an architectonically effective elaboration. Many sections actually appear as fragments of oracles and as reports of secret revelations, and are written in a peculiarly enthusiastic, a solemn, "elevated" style; so much so that the detached reader is apt to feel they have overstepped the bounds of good taste in the direction of affectation and bombast. While often the exposition has an only slightly elevated tone and is pregnant and realistic, we do find in a certain number of passages a passion for the association of ideas which is pushed to an extreme, degenerating into a flight from conceptual reality. Externally, also, many parts are set off from the rest by special titles as more or less independent compositions, and this not without very good reason.

The main part of the Zohar, which is arranged by Pentateuch portions, purports to be an ancient Midrash, and in many details it imitates the form of the ancient midrashic works of the first centuries c.e. On the whole, indeed, it breaks through this form and assumes the quite different one of the medieval sermon. Such extended compositions, constructed on a definite plan, as we find in the Zohar to the length of fifteen or twenty or even forty pages, are quite foreign to the ancient Midrash. Here a different principle of composition obtains. The same is true of the parts called *Midrash ha-Neelam* (The Secret Midrash) and *Sitre Torah* (Secrets of the Torah), which in a large number of Pentateuch portions, especially in the first book, provide parallel pieces to the "main parts."

The Secret Midrash, to be sure, has much to say about Simeon ben Yohai and his circle, but almost completely avoids genuinely mystical and theosophical trains of thought; instead, in its most important sections, it presents radical allegorizations of the patriarchal stories as indicative of the fate of the soul before and after death. These allegories very clearly reveal their kinship to the philosophical homiletic of the 13th century. The Secrets of the Torah, on the other hand, which in the main was composed without the use of the Midrash form or the addition of names, represents the transition from philosophical-eschatological allegory to genuinely mystical exegesis.

The *Idra Rabba* (The Great Assembly) describes, on an excellently constructed plan, the mystical "figure" of the Deity in the symbol of Primal Man, and Simeon ben Yohai treats the same theme a second time in a monologue before his death, an event which is most vividly described in *Idra Zutta* (The Small Assembly). Anonymous "Mishnayot" and "Toseftot," intended as introductions to other longer sections, expound oracles concerning the world and the soul. In *Raya Mehemna* (The Faithful Shepherd), Moses and Rabbi Simeon converse about the hidden reasons for the commandments. The *Tikkunim* again give a detailed interpretation of the first section of the Pentateuch, and thus we have more than a total of ten great and small parts that are evidently separate units. It is no wonder, therefore, that the question of the unity of the Zohar has found very uncertain answers.

ORIGIN AND AUTHORSHIP

While the different points of view in Zohar criticism cannot be fully gone into here, the present status of research can, at any rate, be briefly summarized. The most radical opinion was put forth by Heinrich Graetz. He declared all parts of the Zohar without exception to be the work of the Spanish kabbalist Moses de Leon, who died in 1305, and the great historian emptied the vials of an exceedingly vehement wrath over him. Very few reputations have come down to posterity from the school of Graetz in so battered and pitiable a state as has de Leon's. Far from recognizing the genius that must have been at work in the Zohar, if it was the production of a single man, Graetz saw in it only deception and charlatanism.

In contrast to this view, the Zohar has been regarded, especially in the preceding generation, as a work altogether without unity, or else as one that grew anonymously in the course of time, and in which the most varied and often contradictory forces of the kabbalistic movement found expression. In either case, Moses de Leon was in this view regarded as the redactor of ancient writings and fragments, to which he may perhaps have added something of his own. The theory that "primitive" sources and documents have been preserved in the Zohar, although admittedly in revised form, is today widespread. Thus the Zohar (and this is undoubtedly what has gone to make this view so attractive though it lacks all proof) would really be, even in its external beginnings, a deposit of the creative folk-spirit and, like the Bible and Talmud, the anonymous work of centuries. And it may be taken as an indication of the enduring influence of the school of Ahad Haam that the lack of proof for this theory—and in its behalf not even the shadow of philological-critical evidence has been brought forward—has in no way seriously hindered its spread. What is plausible can do without proof.

Every attempt to establish, through the working out of exact criteria, that certain layers and parts of the Zohar go back to a time before the middle of the 13th century turns out to be new evidence to the contrary. This fact has been vividly experienced by the present writer. After devoting many years to just such an analysis, he found the unequivocal result to correspond so little to the expectations with which he started out, refuting them in fact so thoroughly, that he ventures to state with assurance the following conclusions.

The Zohar is, in the main, a unified book, although not so unified as Graetz imagined. Among the separate parts there are no strata or ancient material from mystical Midrashim unknown to us; on the contrary, these parts came out of the heads of their authors just as they are, except that many parts are undoubtedly missing, having disappeared from the manuscripts as early as the 14th century. Much of the printed text is wrongly arranged, where the manuscript, however, retains the correct order. Finally, a few shorter pieces were added still later in the 14th century. The separate parts do not relate to a corresponding number of strata or authors, but the whole corpus of Zohar literature was in origin made up of three strata. These, in themselves predominantly unified, are:

1. *Midrash ha-Neelam.*
2. The main part of the Zohar with the *Idra Rabba, Idra Zutta, Sitre Torah* and most of the other short treatises.
3. *Raya Mehemna* and the so-called *Tikkune Zohar,* both of which had a single author.

Certain it is that the author of the third stratum, who had the second before him in completed form and cites it and rather unsuccessfully imitates it, is not the author of the first two. Everything speaks against this being so: the linguistic character of the third, its strongly apocalyptic tendencies, its laborious construction, its divergent views, and its way of using sources. One might perhaps propose the rather hazardous thesis that we are here dealing with the work of the old age and decline of the chief author, whose early talents had left him and who was imitating himself, were it not for the fact that too much of an independent nature inheres in the book *Tikkunim* to make this thesis tenable. This last group of writing was composed around 1300.

The first two strata, on the other hand, are in all probability by a single author, whose development from the composition of the first to the second is still clearly traceable, and thus it becomes gratuitous to assume any break in the identity of the person who stands behind the whole production. The Secret Midrash, which has hitherto been customarily regarded as the latest part of the whole work because of its free use of philosophical terminology as well as its partial use of the Hebrew language, is in all probability the earliest part.

Behind the whole stands the living personality of a mystic who, starting with the philosophical and talmudic education of his time, lets himself be ever more deeply drawn to the mystical and gnostic ideas of the Kabbalah, and finally gives up his philosophical interests altogether, developing instead a truly astonishing genius for mystical homiletics; indeed, half a millennium had to elapse before Jewish literature was again able to show anything comparable. For such is the author of these most important parts of the Zohar—no redactor or collector but a homiletic genius. It was Kabbalah, as it had developed before his time, and having become his spiritual home, which he, with unexpected and impressive power, constructed from out of the text of Scripture and the ancient haggadic motifs of the Midrash.

Thus although his world of thought and concept was not novel, his mystical sources were by no means forgotten tomes and apocrypha from obscure centuries. They were the literature of the Kabbalah to the time of Moses ben Nahman (1195–1270) and his circle, a literature which has been in large part preserved and is today quite well known. The manner in which this Zohar author's mystical world was constructed reveals to us very precisely the only period of time in which he is to be correctly placed in the development of the Kabbalah; in addition to which a whole series of linguistic and factual criteria, quite independent of one another, point to exactly the same time. It was certainly around 1280 that these main parts of the Zohar were composed in Spain by a kabbalist who had not seen Palestine. In ever new guises and externally different literary and stylistic forms this work erupts from an author who seems to have deeply experienced his conversion to kabbalism. But in spite of all the masks which he is fond of putting on, the inner form and the personal style are always identical.

But what about these masks? What about this whole Galilean landscape, which dissolves into unreality, and Rabbi Simeon ben Yohai, his family and friends, and all the other trappings of a Midrash-like finery, in which the author seems to find so much pleasure, as if enjoying himself in the play of fantasy? This flight into pseudonymity and romantic backdrop evoked in the critical writings of the 19th century a literary excitement—angry attacks and moralistic condemnation, as well as a circumspect and sometimes vociferous apologetic—which seems to us today to have been considerably exaggerated. For a long time we have known that literary forgeries represent a flight into anonymity and pseudonymity just as often as they indicate trickery; and not for nothing have we retained the foreign word "pseudepigrapha" to designate in particular a legitimate category of religious literature, by a term devoid of the moralistic undertone of reprobation which echoes in the English word "forgery." Important documents of our religious literature are in this sense forgeries; also, the mystical literature which the author of the Zohar may have read consisted, to a considerable extent, of earlier pseudepigrapha.

We are not even sure whether the author, who handles the technique of pseudepigraphy with so much virtuosity and permits the persons of his dialogue a profusion of invented book titles and citations, took the literary form of the kabbalistic pseudepigrapha very seriously. Certainly, in a whole series of imitations of the Zohar which appeared during the first hundred years after its publication, it is clear that their authors did not by any means take the masquerade for the real thing. The masquerade served as a welcome means of letting the chance name of an author who found himself in possession of secret wisdom disappear behind his material, and if the framework is sometimes overdecorated by wilful or, it may be, reckless hands—and the Zohar is the most important but by far not the only example of such love of masquerade in Jewish literature—still this was only an added touch. Only later were these things more crudely conceived, when the disguise became a historical reality.

How playfully the author of the Zohar himself used this form is shown by the noteworthy fact that together with this book he composed still other shorter pseudepigraphic works, of which one, the so-called "Testament of Rabbi Eliezer the Great," has enjoyed the good fortune of being among the most widely circulated Jewish folk-books, although its true origin has gone generally unrecognized. Graetz, indeed, has pictured Moses de Leon to us as forging the Zohar out of greed for profit, in order to make money out of the gullible rich after the books published under his own name had ceased to yield him sufficient gain. This storybook figure of a cunning rogue would be unacceptable to historical criticism even if we did not have conclusive proof that the main part of the Zohar was in existence before 1286, the year that Moses de Leon wrote his "own" first book, which was entirely based upon the Zohar. This does not, of course, exclude the possibility of his having written the Zohar himself previous to that year.

But was Moses de Leon in fact the author of this very Zohar, as even his own contemporaries long ago suspected? We may now say with a fair amount of philological certainty that Moses de Leon must indeed be considered the actual author of the book. True, while much former evidence bolstering that hypothesis has been disproved, there has now come to light certain entirely new evidence to speak decisively for Moses de Leon's authorship. This much is certain: Moses de Leon was in possession of the original work and circulated it from 1280 on, so that a countryman of his, Isaac ibn Sahula of Guadalajara read The Secret Midrash as early as 1281. From 1286 on Moses de Leon composed his "own" writings in very considerable number. These books reveal an author who lives and moves wholly in the specific world of the Zohar and not merely in the general world of the contemporary Kabbalah, so that we have only the choice of saying either that he entirely surrendered himself to the stronger personality of the nameless author of the Zohar, to the extent of giving up his own personal traits, or that he himself was the author. For the latter view there is a noteworthy chronological indication. Up until recently, no one knew how old Moses de Leon was when he began to write, or whether it was at all possible to fit into his "pre-history," before he began to write under his own name, those ten to twenty years which must have been at the very least required for the conception of a work of the kind to which the first two strata of the Zohar belong. But before the First World War, there was found in Moscow a manuscript which by a strange coincidence was none other than one of the scripts of Maimonides' "Guide to the Perplexed," and had been written for Moses de Leon in 1264. These twenty "empty" years (1264 to 1286) preceding his public appearance fit in very strikingly indeed with the period of the origin of the Zohar, which has been determined through quite different connections and criteria. Would not the path that led from the reading of the "Guide to the Perplexed" to the eschatological mysticism of Moses de Leon's "Book of the Rational Soul" be the very one which was described above as that of the inner development of the Zohar's author, from half-philosophical allegory to the mystical-theosophical interpretation of Scripture? We may say with certitude that no one of the other Spanish kabbalists of that period who are within our ken and appear before us with their individual spiritual traits can be brought into the question as a possible author of the Zohar. Neither Abraham Abulafia nor Moses of Burgos, neither Jacob of Segovia nor Joseph Gikatila shows that unmistakable physiognomy. And whoever is unwilling to believe in the Great Unknown who has so successfully eluded all attempts to trace him, must give his adherence to Moses de Leon, if he wishes to succeed in the reconstruction of one of the most significant and clearly marked figures of Jewish religious history.

Something must here be said about the language of the Zohar, which has proved to be one of the most important factors in its influence. The sustained chiaroscuro of this peculiar Zohar-Aramaic has overlaid with a venerable patina and a luster of restrained enthusiasm ideas which, if they had been expressed in the sober Hebrew of the 13th century, would have had to speak by themselves; in the form which they assumed, they have, one might say, found their native idiom. This linguistic achievement is the more admirable in that the medieval Hebrew, as is evident to a keen eye, shows through the Aramaic on page after page, in word order, syntax and terminology; and the more admirable also, considering that the Aramaic vocabulary of the author evidences a curious poverty and simplicity. As soon as one has read thirty pages of the original, one knows the language of the whole book well enough, and in this same respect it is astonishing with what modest resources so much has been expressed and so great an effect has been achieved. Often enough the exact understanding of a passage in the Zohar is dependent upon a retranslation into the Hebrew of the contemporary Kabbalah, and Moses de Leon's writings above all quickly give the key to many passages. A good many mystical concepts are expressed rather arbitrarily in new word-formations, which in many cases have arisen from corrupted forms of talmudic words in medieval manuscripts, or from similar misunderstandings.

How to Decipher a Zoharic Text

In Western tradition, when we study any given theology, we usually find ourselves examining an attempt to think systematically about God's manifestations, or His acts, or His words. That is, when theologians write, they try to make sense out of what God has done and/or what God has said. Theologians do not usually try to tell us what is going on inside the mind of God. Theologians do not usually try to tell us of the conflicts that God experienced in creating the world, or of the tensions within God as He guides and directs the world through His Providence. Theologians try, rather, to systematize, in some way, the exoteric doctrines or beliefs of a tradition. Similarly, those religious leaders responsible for defining the practice of the community do not tell us of the inner workings of the personhood of God. Rather, they regulate and interpret behavior for the community. They teach people what to do. This tendency to avoid talking about God in strongly anthropopathic terms (i.e., in terms that attribute human feelings to God) took especially deep root in the Middle Ages in all the Western religious traditions because of the influence of Greek philosophy, which thought of God as perfect, unchanging, unsusceptible to the vagaries of human existence.

The Zohar represents a forceful break with this way of thinking of God, for the Zohar is "theosophy" (or "theosophical gnosis"). By this I mean that the Zohar purports not only to interpret God's revealed words and acts, but also to describe the inner workings of God's mind. The Zohar purports not only to describe the divine realms of the angels, spirits, etc., but to tell us of the workings of the very personality of God. It claims to describe the various, often conflicting, elements that comprise the consciousness of God. This will seem strange, even preposterous, to the modern reader, yet it is so. The Zohar teaches that personal consciousness is of the essence of God, that personal consciousness is the common element in man and God—the image of God in which man was created.

To decipher a Zoharic text, then, the Western and modern reader must suspend all presuppositions about the nature of God as a perfect, immobile Being and must engage the text as an essay in the psychology of God. Just what *is* God like? What kind of personality *does* He have? He has, according to the tradition, left a good record of His thoughts (the Bible) and of His acts (creation and history). Why not try to develop a "psychology of God"? The Zohar presupposes that this can be done, and does it. The reader must accept the presupposition and then examine the results for their religious meaning (even if they cannot be "verified" in any "objective" or "scientific" way). The cautious student may prefer to treat this system as a symbolic system or as a mythic structure, yet he should be aware that, for the Zohar and its readers, this is real. It is (esoteric) truth.

What, then, are the main elements in the psychology of God? The Zohar uses the word *sefirot* (sing. *sefira*) to describe the basic components of the personality of God (and, and by implication, of man). This word is the same as that used in the Sefer Yetsira, yet there the sefirot were outside of God (extradeical), while in the Zohar the sefirot are inside God (intradeical). They are part of Him. We do not know exactly how the author of the Zohar came to this conception of God, or to this use of the word *sefirot,* but the usage exists and it is clear.

The Zohar teaches, then, that there are ten sefirot. They are known individually and collectively by several names and by several sets of symbols. They can be called: rivers, pillars, heavens, supports, worlds, aspects, borders, hosts, steps, crowns, clothing, fountains, streams, gates, days, colors, etc. They can be organized according to groupings of the various divine Names. As a collective, they can be referred to as: a garden, a field, a tree, or a Primal Man. The sefirot also have generally accepted names, as follows: Keter, Hokhma, Bina, Gevura (sometimes, Din), Hesed, Tiferet, Nesah, Hod, Yesod, and Malkhut. It is not entirely clear whether these accepted names always have the same meanings and connotations. Yet as aspects of the personality of God, the ten sefirot can be construed as followed:

> Keter: God's transcendent, or pure, royalty
> Hokhma: the wisdom, or mind, of God
> Bina: God's (intuitive) understanding
> Gevura: God's transcendent, or pure, power
> Hesed: God's transcendent, or pure, grace (unmerited love)
> Tiferet: God's active royalty; His Kingship
> Nesah: God's active grace
> Hod: God's active power
> Yesod: God's righteous power (confluence of the above sefirot)
> Malkhut: God's engaged royalty; His Providence (connection with all
> the lower realms); His Presence or Face

The characteristics listed and the metaphors used to describe the realm of the sefirot suggest that this is not a static realm. Rather, as the reader may already have surmised, these characteristics are interactive. Their relationships are dynamic. An energy pervades this system, and this energy flows from sefira to sefira, activating and intensifying its characteristics as it moves. The Zohar conceives of the personality, or consciousness, of God on the model of the dynamic human personality, i.e., as a consciousness that flows and moves within the self, from the inner to the outer aspects of the self and even among the inner and outer aspects. It is strange that a complete understanding of the Zohar may only come after the insights of modern psychology have opened our eyes to the complexity and depth of the human personality. Then, perhaps, we will understand more of God's personality, for it is personal consciousness that binds man and God together, according to the Zohar.

To decipher a Zoharic text, then, the reader must memorize the names and sequence of the sefirot, together with their simplest meanings. Three diagrams (Figs. 9, 10, 11) are presented for the reader to study. The commentary to the texts will use the one labeled "The Sefirotic Tree—II" (Fig. 11).

To decipher a Zoharic text, the reader must also know that in Western tradition, mixing one's metaphors is considered bad style. Not so in the Zohar. There, mixing metaphors is considered an art. And so, in any given passage, one must expect to find the same sefira referred to with several designations. One can even expect the entire realm of the sefirot and the dynamic flow of divine energy that pulses through that realm to be referred to by the simultaneous use of several symbol-systems. The river beds will contain light. The orchard will contain kings. The Queen will be watered from the deep stream. And so on. This Alice-in-Wonderland quality of Zoharic style is an essential part of the point the author is trying to make, and the reader will want to consider: What *is* the point, and how does this style help the author to make it?

Finally, to decipher a Zoharic text, the reader must know that each text exists on several levels. There is, first of all, the level of the Biblical text, for the Zohar is a commentary to the Bible. The reader must identify the problem in the Biblical text that is the springboard for the Zoharic homily. The modern reader, using critical scholarly method, will frequently see no problem. It must then be kept in mind that the author of the Zohar accepts the classic rabbinic position of the unitary and divine authorship of the Bible, and hence the rule that there is no needless repetition of words in the Bible. All such stylistic parallelisms, therefore, must contain some hidden meaning, and it is often this assumption that creates a problem for the author of the Zohar, allowing him to develop his insights.

Second, there is the level of the accepted rabbinic interpretation of the passage. Rabbinic tradition frequently interprets Biblical passages in a semi-allegorical mode to refer to God, Israel, Torah, *mitsvot,* etc. This

THE SEFIROTIC TREE—I

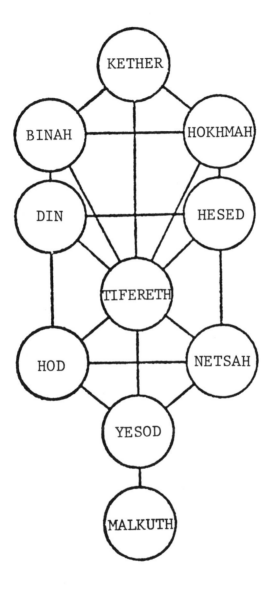

(From Scholem, *Major Trends in Jewish Mysticism*, p. 214.

Fig. 9

PRIMAL MAN

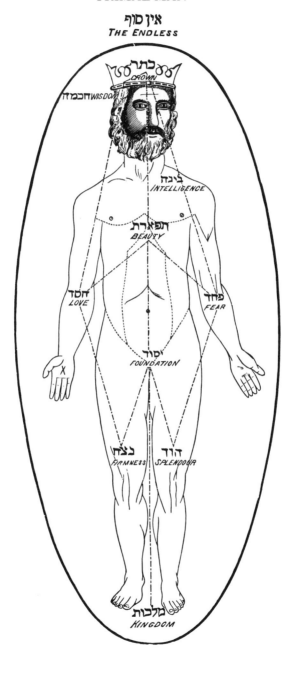

Fig. 10

THE SEFIROTIC TREE—II

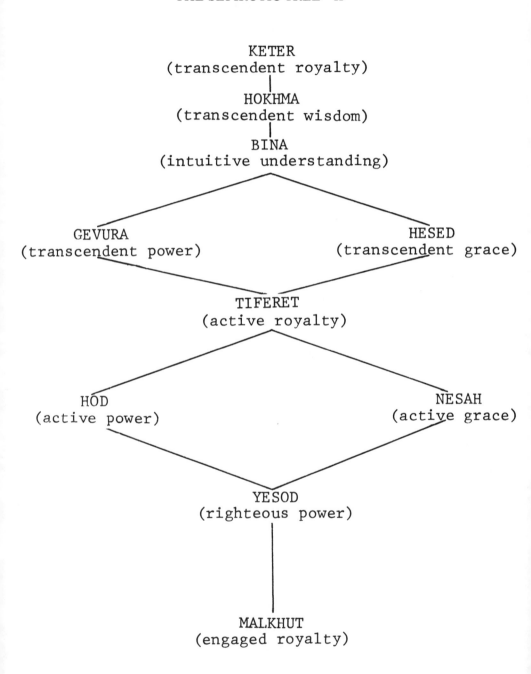

Fig. 11

accepted tradition of commentation allows the casual reader to read through the Zohar and to proclaim that there is nothing very special about its interpretation of the Bible. For most of the text of the Zohar is structured so that it can be read on the commonly accepted rabbinic level of interpretation, without any clear reference to the theosophic ideas that it contains. This is a very clever and artful clothing of insights in a seemingly innocuous commentary.

The third level of interpretation of a Zoharic text is the actual decipherment of the sefirotic symbolism. For example: "Community of Israel" is a symbol for Malkhut. "Tree of Life" is a symbol for Tiferet. "Shekhina" is a symbol for Malkhut. "Most Hidden One" is a symbol for Keter (sometimes, Hokhma). "Sea" is a symbol for Bina (sometimes, Malkhut). And so on. A list of the symbolic correspondences would fill several pages of print, and the reader must follow the commentary and develop his own instincts. (I. Tishby, in his *Mishnat ha-Zohar,* 2 vols. [Jerusalem: Bialik Institute, 1961], translates passages of the Zohar into Hebrew and analyzes the symbolism, in Hebrew. The ten-volume *Zohar 'im Sullam* [London, 1970] does much the same.) Having deciphered the sefirotic symbolism, the reader arrives at the fourth level of interpretation—the consideration of the meaning of the text. That is, the reader must try to interpret the nature of the interaction of the sefirot being described: What has happened, in psychological terms? Does the sefirotic interaction described have a true analogy in the workings of human consciousness? And, as the reader's insight into God develops under the guidance of the Zohar, the reader must ask: Is this possible? Can God really contain these elements in Himself? Do the tensions described contradict traditional Jewish theology? Are they heretical in some sense? What does the depiction of God contained in the Zohar say about the nature of reality: divine and mundane? If these passages do not challenge and startle you, you have not understood them.

8

THE PERSONALITY OF GOD

The Rose and the Lily

This text is a beautiful example of a text existing on several levels. The reader must ask: What is the problem in the Biblical verse that permits the author to develop his homily? What is the overt symbolic interpretation of the text? Then the reader must decipher the sefirotic symbolism of the text. Finally, the reader must try to evaluate the meaning of the text in its deepest psychological and spiritual terms. Note, too, the artful interweaving of Biblical texts in the homily.

Rabbi Shimon opened his discourse: "I am a Rose of Sharon, a Lily of the Valleys" [Song of Songs 2:1]. How beloved is the Community of Israel before the Holy One, blessed be He. For He praises her and she always praises Him. And how great is the store of praises and song she has put up for him. Happy is the lot of Israel who grasp the portion of the holy fate as it says . . .

Because she flowers splendidly in the Garden of Eden, the Community of Israel is called "Rose of Sharon"; also, because she chants and praises the high King; also because her desire is to be watered from the deep stream which is the source of all spiritual rivers as it is said, "The Sharon is like the desert" [Isaiah 33:9]. Because, [however], she is found at the deepest places, she is called "Lily of the Valleys." What are these deep places? They are: "from the deep places, I have called You" [Psalm 130:1].

[Another interpretation:] "Rose of Sharon" [refers to] the place of the watering from which deep rivers flow always, without stopping. "Lily of the Valleys" [refers to] the place which is the deepest of all, the most hidden of all.

Come and see: At first, she is a green rose with green petals. Afterwards, she becomes a lily with two colors: red and white.—A lily also has six petals. And a lily [*shoshana*] changes [*sheni'at*] her colors from hue to hue.—The lily, which was first a rose, is [again] called a rose when she is ready to unite with the King. After she clings to the King, with those [special] kisses, she is [again] called a lily. [III:107a]*

The Biblical text cited here is a line from one of the love poems that comprise the Song of Songs. In this poem, the woman is speaking, and she compares herself to a rose and to a lily. Ostensibly she does this because, being in love, she perceives herself as beautiful and radiant (i.e., fragrant) like a flower. The Biblical text probably intends the rose and the lily to be parallel images, with no deeper meaning to be ascribed to them. The author of the Zohar, assuming that literary parallelism is not simply art-form but an allusion to a deeper meaning, understands the rose and the lily to have two different connotations. A rose is, after all, not a lily, and if Scripture uses two metaphors, two meanings must have been intended. What, then, is the hidden meaning?

The rabbinic tradition, from early times, understood the Song of Songs as an allegory of the relationship between Israel and God, the lover being God and the beloved being the Jewish people. (Christianity developed a parallel interpretation, with the lover being God and the beloved being the Church.) The text can be understood on this level as depicting the reciprocal relationship between God and the people. It is, then, a development of the covenant theology of the Bible in poetic imagery. Parts of this text (e.g., the changing colors of the flowers and the deep-stream imagery) are mildly incomprehensible, but these passages can be glossed over with the admission of poetic license. To fully understand the passage and its revolutionary implications, one must decipher the sefirotic symbolism.

The sefirotic symbolism is as follows: The "Community of Israel" stands for Malkhut, and the "Holy One, blessed be He" stands for Tiferet. Reread the first paragraph, substituting the names of the sefirot for their symbols. The result is that Malkhut is always praising Tiferet and Tiferet is always praising Malkhut.

Moving to the fourth level of interpretation, the consideration of the meaning of the sefirotic symbolism, the reader must recall that the sefirot represent aspects of the inner consciousness of God. What, then, does it mean to say that God's engaged royalty and His active royalty interact? What does it mean to say that the center of God's personality "praises" the outer aspects of it, and vice versa? that God's Presence interacts with His Kingship?

---

*The number in brackets at the end of the reading refers to the source in the standard edition of the Zohar. For a slightly different rendering, see G. Scholem, *Zohar: The Book of Splendor* (New York: Schocken Books, 1972), p. 118.

An appreciation of human psychology can lead us in a productive direction, for we understand human consciousness to be made up of inner and outer aspects. We understand that each of us has an inner person, an inner core of strength and judgmental power, and that each of us also has an outer face through which we deal with the world around us. We think before we act. We feel before we show it. We lie to the outside world but try not to do it to ourselves. We yield externally, but not internally, to certain kinds of pressures. We, too, have a Malkhut (a Face, a Providence) and a Tiferet (an inner domain of active being). So, too, with God, according to the Zohar. Furthermore, our social interface with reality often reinforces our inner selves, and the reverse—our inner selves often give strength to our presented self-images. That is, the inner and outer aspects of our being interact with one another. They "praise" (and "criticize") one another. So, too, with God. His Malkhut praises His Tiferet, and vice versa.

The meaning of the first paragraph is, then, clear: the inner and outer aspects of God's being interact with one another. How far we have come from the Song of Songs! How far we have come even from the semi-allegorical level of the rabbinic tradition! Incidentally, who is the "Israel" who is happy when it "grasps the portion of the holy fate"?

The second paragraph goes on to expound the difference between the imagery of the rose and that of the lily. (Remember the assumption about literary parallelism.) Three reasons are given why Malkhut is called a rose and one reason why it is called a lily. The sefirotic symbolism is as follows: The "Garden of Eden" is the realm of the sefirot. The "Community of Israel" is again Malkhut, and the "high King" is Tiferet. The "deep stream" is Yesod. The interpretation is as follows: Malkhut is called a rose because it flowers in the realm of the sefirot (i.e., it is the flower, the beautiful end-product, of the flow and development of the sefirotic realm). It is also called a rose (Heb. *havaselet ha-sharon*) because it sings the praise (Heb. *shara*) of Tiferet. This is a pun on two roots which are probably not at all related. It is also called a rose because it yearns to receive the flow of divine energy from the sefira immediately above it, Yesod (see Figs. 9–11). Here too a play on words between *sharon* and the root *shry* ("to water") is intended. Malkhut can also be called a lily, however, when Malkhut is seen not as a blossoming flower, which is lavishly watered and which praises God (note how easy and effective it is to mix metaphors), but when it is seen as sunken in the depths, i.e., as distraught and oppressed. When Malkhut, which is at the bottom of the sefirotic flow, is in despair, it calls out to Tiferet. In this aspect, it is a lily and not a rose.

This last image deserves a moment of attention at level four of interpretation. What does it mean to say that Malkhut can praise Tiferet on the one hand, but that there are times when Malkhut cries out in despair to Tiferet (as the verse in Psalms says)? Again, the analogy from human psychology is helpful. Our outer selves sometimes reinforce our inner selves, but sometimes our outer selves do get depressed. Our self-image is sometimes positive and sometimes negative. In either case, it must seek out our inner self—to praise it or to draw strength from it.

The third paragraph contains a good lesson in method, for the symbols appear to be the same, but the interpretation is quite different. One begins with "the most hidden of all," which almost always stands for Hokhma. Thus, the "Lily of the Valleys" stands, in this paragraph, for Hokhma. The next sefira (down) is Bina which is a passage, or funnel, through which the divine flow must pass. Hence, the "Rose of Sharon" must stand for Bina, in this paragraph.

The fourth paragraph interweaves the symbolism of lily and rose, of color, of change, and of number. It is complex but not impossible to decipher. The reader must simply realize that both images refer to Malkhut and that the lily image is the unstable, dynamic aspect of Malkhut while the rose is the stable, fulfilled aspect thereof. The interpretation, then, is as follows: Malkhut is first a rose (i.e., stable), symbolized by the color green, which itself symbolizes a balanced mixture of the qualities of power and grace. Malkhut then becomes a lily (i.e., unstable), symbolized by being an irregular mixture of two colors, red and white, which symbolize the power and grace of God. In this unstable aspect, Malkhut is also symbolized by the changing of colors (with another pun on unrelated Semitic roots). The six petals are the six sefirot above Malkhut in the sefirotic chain (see Figs. 9–11). Finally the passage explains to us the "life cycle" of Malkhut. It starts out stable and fulfilled (rose). It becomes destabilized (lily). It stabilizes (rose) just before union with Tiferet. And it reaches dynamic fulfillment (lily) when the divine energy ("special kisses," cf. Song of Songs 1:2) unites it with Tiferet.

What does all this mean on the fourth level of interpretation? The passage is telling us that God's Providence is not always stable, that it appears to change according to circumstances which are not made clear in this passage. At times God's Face to man and the world is stable and beautiful like a rose, but at times it is unstable and changing like the colors of a lily. This realization is not, on the surface, very strange, for the problem of the irregularity of God's Providence has occupied the minds of men for a long time. But if we examine a little more deeply, we note that the passage really says, *not* that God's Providence *appears* unstable, but that it *is* unstable— i.e., that in the inner workings of God, there is an element (Malkhut) which is God's Face to the cosmos, and this element can actually be destabilized. The passage does not, however, tell us how this happens (see below, page 143). The passage also teaches us that this unstable element in God can be stabilized. It does not, however, tell us how this happens either (see below, page 149). But the passage clearly does interpret God in a deeply human way as having an aspect of Himself which, by its nature, is not stable but which, by its nature, can also be stabilized. God's consciousness contains an aspect which knows unity with its own inner forces but which is also subject to the vagaries of forces acting upon it. To the traditional theologian, these are very strange ideas. To the philosopher, they are preposterous. Yet for the author of the Zohar, they are central to our understanding of God. What do you think?

The Similitude of God

In this passage, the author of the Zohar deals with the question, Just how much *can* we know of God? Theologically, this is a very important question because Judaism has always understood God to be, in some very basic way, unknowable. He is the Creator, and His knowledge and perspective on existence must be categorically different from that of flesh and blood. Yet the Zohar claims to expound the workings of the inner life of God. Hence the author of the Zohar must confront this question. The problem is also important psychologically, for one can legitimately ask, Do we ever know all there is to know of another person? Is there not some internal reserve of unknowability even in the people we know most intimately? What *is* the interplay between unknowability and knowability in man and in God?

To resolve this problem, the author of the Zohar seeks out two verses which speak of the "similitude" (Heb. *temuna*) of God. One verse denies that man can perceive God's similitude, while the other asserts it. Watch carefully his solution.

If one should ask: Is it not written, "For you saw no manner of similitude" [Deuteronomy 4:15], the answer would be: Truly, it *was* granted us to behold Him in a similitude for it [also] says, "And the similitude of the Lord does he behold" [Numbers 12:8]. Yet God was not revealed in any similitude which He created and formed by His signs. Therefore it is written, "To whom, then, will you liken Me that I be compared? To whom will you compare God and what likeness will you accord Him? [Isaiah 40:25,18]. Furthermore, even "that similitude" does not remain in its place but descends to rule the creatures, extending itself over them, appearing to each one of them as each can grasp it, as it is written, "And by the hand of the prophets can I be likened" [Hosea 12:11]. Hence He says, Although I represent Myself in your image, to whom will you compare Me that I be compared?

Before God created image in the universe and shaped form, He was unique, with neither form nor likeness. Hence, if one seeks knowledge

126

of Him before creation, when He had no image, one is forbidden to imagine Him in any kind of form or image—not by His letter Hey or by His letter Yod [two letters of the Tetragrammaton], nor even by His [complete] holy Name, nor by letter or point of any kind. Thus, "For you saw no manner of similitude" means, You beheld nothing [which could be imagined] in likeness or in similitude.

But when He had created the image of the Chariot of Supernal Man, He descended and became known by the appellation YHVH so as to be apprehended by His attributes, in each particular one. Hence He [caused Himself to be] named El, Elohim, Shaddai, Sevaot, and Eheyeh so that men might seek knowledge of Him in each of His divine attributes, [making manifest] that the world is guided by grace and justice in accordance with man's deeds. If His light had not been shed over His creatures, how could men have apprehended Him? Indeed, the words could not have been said, "The whole universe is full of His glory" [Isaiah 6:3].

[However,] woe to the man who compares God with any [single] attribute, even if it be one of His own, and the less so with any human being, "whose foundation is in the dust" [Job 4:19] and who is but a disintegrating vessel. Rather, [our] likening of Him is proportionate to His presence in that attribute and in creation. If He withdraws from it, there is neither attribute nor likeness nor form. Such is the case with the sea, whose waters lack form and likeness, attaining these only when they are spread over the vessel of the earth. [II:42b]*

The solution to the problem of the contradictory verses and the answer to the question about the ultimate knowability of God begin, for the author of the Zohar, in the rabbinic assumption about literary parallelism—that such parallelism alludes to a deeper meaning and is not an art-form of Biblical Hebrew. Working with this assumption, the resolution of both problems is clear and relatively easy. God was unknown before Creation, and that aspect of Him cannot be known even by exploring the meaning of His Name or its letters. After Creation, however, He chose to reveal Himself to man and He made known His various Names and/or attributes. Finally, to identify His Names and/or attributes with Him, with His essence, would be wrong, for they are only labels, expressions of an unknowable essence behind the word. This resolution is classic. It is simple. It is orthodox. And the passage can be read on this rabbinic level without further comment. To understand its theosophical meaning, we must go further. We must decipher the sefirotic symbolism, and then we must evaluate the meaning of that symbolism.

---

*For a slightly different rendering, see Scholem, *Zohar,* pp. 77–78.

To decipher the sefirotic symbolism, the reader must know that "similitude" (Heb. *temuna*) is used in two senses by the author of the Zohar—first, in a nonsefirotic sense, to mean "an image," "a likeness"; and second, in a sefirotic sense, to refer to Tiferet. The reader must also know that the Tetragrammaton is also used in two senses—first, in a general sense, to refer to any of the sefirot and/or to the entire realm of sefirot; and second, to refer to Tiferet. The Hebrew letter Yod is the first letter of the Tetragrammaton and stands for Hokhma, while the Hebrew letter Hey is the second letter of the Tetragrammaton and stands for Bina. The "Chariot of Supernal Man" is the realm of the sefirot. Reread the passage and try to decipher it yourself before reading further.

The first paragraph teaches that the term "similitude of God" can refer to three sefirot depending on the context: the "unperceivable similitude" is Keter, the "perceivable similitude before it descends" is Tiferet, and the "perceivable similitude after it descends to 'rule' and to be grasped" is Malkhut. Note that according to Numbers 12:8 (supported by the verse from Hosea), only Moses was privileged to perceive the "similitude," while the other prophets perceived some lesser likeness of God. This is the classical doctrine of the superiority of the prophecy of Moses. The author of the Zohar preserves this dogma by interpreting that Moses perceived the "undescended similitude" (Tiferet) while the other prophets perceived the "descended similitude" (Malkhut). We have here, then, a carefully articulated theory of the three-stage knowability of God which "resolves" an apparent contradiction in Scripture, which utilizes sefirotic symbolism, and which also preserves the classical rabbinic doctrine of the superiority of the prophecy of Moses.

The second paragraph tells us that Keter (? the God beyond Keter, if there is such an idea), being "beyond" Hokhma—i.e., beyond knowledge—is unknowable. Keter, the most transcendent aspect of God, cannot be grasped even by reference to Yod (Hokhma, knowledge) or to Hey (Bina, intuitive understanding), and certainly not by any combination of any of the other characteristics of God's consciousness. However, as the third paragraph teaches, when God created the realm of the sefirot, He defined Himself, using certain characteristics (each of which corresponds to a Name of God). Here the Tetragrammaton is synonymous with "similitude," and Tiferet is meant. It, together with the other sefirot (Names of God), defines the consciousness of God. They are His attributes, His Names. They define His knowability. They are His content. They are what one can know. Taken together, then, these two paragraphs teach that there is an aspect of God which is beyond knowing (Keter, "similitude" in the first sense), an aspect that can be known through intellectual knowledge (Hokhma), an aspect that can be known through intuitive understanding (Bina), a central attribute (Tiferet, YHVH, "similitude" in the second sense), five other attributes (see Figs. 9–11, Malkhut being "similitude" in the third sense), and that these sefirot constitute the "universe" whose wholeness is filled with the glory of God. It is, furthermore, this flow of self-definition that enables us to know God, and should He choose to suspend the flow, everything would revert back to unknowability.

What does this mean? How shall we understand the relationship of unknowability to knowability in God and man? There are several insights worth noting. First, the Zohar teaches that the innermost core of God (and man) is unknowable—not unknown but unknowable. The inner core of man (and God) is simply not describable in any kind of language whatsoever. It is not accessible through any systematic knowledge or any insight whatsoever. We cannot grasp the very being of someone else (or of God). We can only grasp his qualities as mediated through our intellect and intuition. Second, self-revelation is a process of self-definition. God (and man) defines Himself. He lets Himself be known. Furthermore, He lets His inner qualities, as well as His "Face," be known. He exposes Himself to the human mind and to human intuition. Yet the process of self-exposure in man (and God) is itself a definition of certain qualities and their interaction. These qualities are the "names" we have. They are the epithets by which we are known. They are the language by which people know us and describe us. These qualities are manifest in our behavior (guidance of the world around us). Or, to word it differently but say the same thing: Our behavior testifies to our qualities. Third, should we (or God) withdraw from this process of self-definition, we would halt communication with others, and we ourselves would return to formlessness. Identity is definition. Self-consciousness is content-ful communication. Self-revelation is knowability. Being, however, is beyond identity and knowability. Note that the author of the Zohar refers to this process of self-definition as "creation." One creates one's identity. God creates His identity. "Creation" is the willed flowing-forth of the sefirot. This is a very new definition of the word *creation* in Jewish theology.

The Water and the Vessels

We have seen that the Zohar depicts God as knowable in His inner consciousness, though not in His innermost being. We have also seen that the knowable aspects of God are said to have proceeded from Him in an act of self-revelation, called by the author of the Zohar "creation." How did these aspects of God's consciousness proceed from Him? In what order? This passage attempts an answer to that question. By following the diagrams of the realm of the sefirot (Figs. 9–11), the reader should have no trouble in following the passage. One hint: the word *sea* is used in two senses: to refer to the entire realm of the sefirot and to refer to the third sefira thereof, Bina.

One, is the source of the sea. A current comes forth from it making a revolution which is *yod*. The source is one, and the current makes two. Then the vast basin known as the sea is formed, and it is like a channel dug into the earth. It is filled by the waters issuing from the source, and this sea is the third thing. This vast basin is divided up into seven channels, resembling that number of long tubes, and the waters go from the sea into the seven channels. Together, the source, the current, the sea, and the seven channels make the number ten. If the Creator Who made these tubes should choose to break them, then the waters would return to their source, and only broken vessels would remain dry, without water.

In this same way the Cause of causes has derived the ten aspects of His Being which are known as sefirot, and named Keter the Source, which is a never-to-be-exhausted fountain of light, wherefrom He designates Himself *'eyn sof,* the Infinite. Neither shape nor form has he, and no vessel exists to contain him, nor any means to apprehend him. This is referred to in the words: "Refrain from searching after the things that are too hard for thee, and refrain from seeking for the thing which is hidden from thee" [Ben Sira, as quoted in the Talmud, *Hagigah* 13a].

Then He shaped a vessel diminutive as the letter *Yod,* and filled it from it, and called it Wisdom-gushing Fountain (Hokhma), and called Himself wise on its account. And after, He fashioned a large vessel named sea, and designated it Understanding [Binah] and Himself understanding, on its account. Both wise and understanding is He, in His own essence; whereas Wisdom in itself cannot claim that title, but only through Him Who is wise and has made it full from His fountain; and so Understanding in itself cannot claim that title, but only through Him Who filled it from His own essence, and it would be rendered into an aridity if He were to go from it. In this regard, it is written, "As the waters fall from the sea, and the river is drained dry" [Job 14:11].

Finally, "He smites [the sea] into seven streams" [Isaiah 11:15], that is, He directs it into seven precious vessels, which He calls Greatness, Strength, Glory, Victory, Majesty, Foundation, Sovereignty [the seven lower sefirot]. In each He designates Himself thus: great in Greatness, strong in Strength, glorious in Glory, victorious in Victory, "the beauty of our Maker" in Majesty, righteous in Foundation [cf. Proverbs 10:25]. All things, all vessels, and all worlds does He uphold in Foundation.

In the last, in Sovereignty, He calls Himself King, and [then] His is "the greatness, and the strength, and the glory, and the victory, and the majesty; for all [foundation] that is in heaven and in the earth is Thine; Thine is the sovereignty, O Lord, and Thou art exalted as head above all" [I Chronicles 29:11]. In His power lie all things, be it that He chooses to reduce the number of vessels, or to increase the light issuing therefrom or be it the contrary. But over Him there exists no deity with power to increase or reduce.

Also, He made beings to serve these vessels: each a throne supported by four columns, with six steps to the throne; in all, ten. Altogether, the throne is like the cup of benediction about which ten statements are made [in the Talmud], harmonious with the Torah which was given in Ten words [the Decalogue], and with the Ten Words by which the world was created. [II:42b–43a]*

In this passage, the author of the Zohar tells us how God allowed his consciousness to develop. He speaks of God as separate from the sefirot, as a being who allows the sefirot to flow from Him. This narrative usage may be only a literary device or the author of the Zohar may be trying to define an active, willing God outside of (beyond) the realm of the sefirot. I have tried to capture this narrative usage by capitalizing the words for God when they refer to the narrative figure.

---

*Trans. by G. Scholem, *Zohar,* pp. 79–80.

The passage is rather straightforward, and only a few end-notes are necessary to clarify some points. In the first paragraph: Note that should the vessels break, the flow of energy returns to God. It does not spill out. We shall see that later Kabbalists did not agree. In the second paragraph: Note that Keter and 'Eyn Sof are regarded as synonymous. The author of the Zohar is not consistent in this symbolism, and later Kabbalists rejected it. Also note the reference to the being beyond the sefirot as the "Cause of causes." This is a clear indication of a medieval origin for this text. Such terms do not exist in second-century texts. In the third paragraph: Note that the letter Yod (Hokhma) is the first letter of the Tetragrammaton (which can, on occasion, symbolize the whole realm of the sefirot as it does here); also that it is written by making a little curlicue ("revolution") with a pen. In the fourth paragraph: Note that no quality, no description of reality, has any existence except through the presence of the divine flow of energy in it. All existence is contingent, as the philosophers put it. The fifth paragraph uses the verse in Chronicles, which is actually part of David's blessing to the people before he dies, to define the sefirot as follows: "Yours, O YHVH (the realm of the sefirot), are greatness (Heb. *gedula,* an alternate term for Hesed), power (Heb. *gevura* / sefira of the same name), glory (Heb. *tiferet*), victory (Heb. *nesah*), majesty (Heb. *hod*), for all (Heb. *kol,* alternate term for Yesod) is in the heaven and the earth (the realm of the sefirot). Yours, O YHVH, is sovereignty (Heb. *mamlakha,* from the same root as Malkhut) . . ." All the seven lower sefirot are, thus, accounted for.

The last paragraph contains several problems. The author refers to "thrones" with "columns" and "steps" which "support" each sefira. I do not know what he intends, although he probably is referring to some sort of angelic orders which would be outside the realm of God's inner being and which would execute His will (i.e., "support" Him). At the end, the author associates the ten sefirot, each of which has ten supporting elements, with the ten statements made about the cup of benediction (Talmud, *Berakhot* 51a), the Decalogue, and the Ten Words by which the world was created (Mishna, *Pirkei Avot,* chap. 4).

The Luminous Glass

This text is very complicated because it deals with prophecy and mysticism, because it deals with two very problematic Biblical verses, and because it unites differing symbol-systems in an exceptionally complicated way. The author begins by asking what the word *appeared* means when applied to God, and he receives (or gives) an answer which explains that God never reveals His true self, that He does reveal different aspects of His personality to different people, and that the mystic can perceive some of these aspects of God.

The key to the symbolism is as follows: One symbol-set deals with colors. There are three types of colors. (1) There are invisible colors which no human may comprehend. (2) There are invisible colors which are hidden and which are subsequently made manifest. This manifestation has two levels: (a) that of Moses and the mystic, and (b) that of the Patriarchs and the mystic. The first two types (1 and 2a) are radiant colors but not the last. Deciphered, type 1 is (probably) Hokhma and Bina, type 2a is Tiferet, and type 2b is Malkhut. Another symbol-set deals with the Divine Names: El Shaddai is Malkhut, and YHVH is Tiferet. Another symbol-set deals with firmaments: the radiant firmament is Tiferet, the nonradiant firmament is Malkhut. The firmaments contain, or reflect, the colors. Another symbol-set deals with a glass, or crystal, through which God is perceived: the luminous glass is Tiferet, the nonluminous glass is Malkhut. Another symbol-set deals with light. The artistry of the passage is in the interweaving of the symbol systems.

Rabbi Shimon was sitting one day with his son, Rabbi Elazar, and Rabbi Abba was also with him. Rabbi Elazar said: In this verse in which it is written, "And I appeared to Abraham, to Isaac, and to Jacob [as] 'El Shaddai but [by] my Name, YHVH, I was not known to them" [Exodus 6:3], what is [the meaning of] "and I appeared"? The verse should say "and I spoke." Rabbi Shimon said to him: Elazar, my son, this is highly esoteric doctrine.

133

Come and see. There are colors which are visible, and there are colors which are invisible, and both are highly esoteric doctrine of the faith which [ordinary] humans do not know and into which they have no insight. Furthermore, no person merited [comprehension] even of those colors which are visible until the Patriarchs came and comprehended them. Therefore the verse says, "and I appeared to Abraham . . ." [i.e., that] they [the Patriarchs] saw those colors which had been made manifest. What are these colors which were made manifest? They are the colors [seen in] El Shaddai. They are the envisionment of the higher colors, for they are visible while the higher colors are hidden and invisible, and no person has comprehended them [the higher colors] except Moses. Therefore the verse says, "But [by] my Name YHVH, I was not known to them." I did not reveal myself to them [the Patriarchs] as the higher colors. And lest you say that the Patriarchs had no knowledge of them [the higher colors at all, know that they knew of them] from [their comprehension] of those colors which had been made manifest.

This part of the text teaches that before the Patriarchs, there was no real comprehension of the sefirot (except, presumably, for Adam in the Garden of Eden [see below, p. 143]). Then, just as God had progressively allowed His own inner being to flow forth, He progressively allowed His inner being to be comprehended by man. The Partiarchs were the first worthy people; they comprehended Malkhut (the visible or manifested colors) although they had a premonition of the upper sefirot (the invisible colors). Then Moses, who was more meritorious, came along, and he comprehended Tiferet (the invisible colors). All this corresponds with the verse in Exodus 6:3 that Malkhut (El Shaddai) preceded Tiferet (YHVH) in the self-revelation of God. The meaning of this sefirotic symbolism (the fourth level of interpretation) is that self-revelation is a gradual process and that it follows inner self-articulation. Note, however, that Moses outranks the Patriarchs in his comprehension of God.

Having expounded a verse (from Exodus) using two symbol-systems: the visible/invisible colors and the Divine Names (El Shaddai/YHVH), the author of the Zohar now takes on a new verse (from Daniel) and two new symbol-systems: that of the radiant/nonradiant colors and that of the firmaments.

It is written, "And the intelligent ones shall be as radiant as the radiance of the firmament while those who justify the masses [will be as bright] as the stars forever" [Daniel 12:3]. "The intelligent ones shall be radiant"—who are these "intelligent ones"? That wise man who intuits on his own things which one may not speak with the mouth is

called an "intelligent one." "As the radiance of the firmament"—
what is this "firmament"? It is the "firmament" of Moses, which
stands in the middle, and its radiance is hidden and unrevealed. It
stands above the "nonradiant firmament" in which colors are visible,
but these [visible] colors, although they are visible, they do not have
the radiance of the [invisible] hidden colors.

In this paragraph, the author of the Zohar teaches that there are two
firmaments: one which is radiant, and one which is nonradiant. The radiant
firmament "stands in the middle," that is, it is Tiferet (see Figs. 9–11), and
it is the one perceived by Moses. The nonradiant firmament is Malkhut, and
it contains colors which are visible but not radiant. I think that even in
common English usage we would say that "radiant" colors were
"superior" to "nonradiant" colors, just as "invisible" colors would be
"superior" to "visible" colors. If we were to try to integrate the
symbol-sets used so far (on the principle of things-standing-for-the-same-
thing-stand-for-each-other), we would conclude that there are three stages
in the self-revelation of God. Before the Patriarchs, the sefirot were
unknown. After the Patriarchs, Malkhut (the visible colors/El Shaddai/
nonradiant firmament) could be comprehended. And after Moses, Tiferet
(the invisible colors/YHVH/radiant firmament) could be comprehended.

The most important point, however, remains to be made, and the author
of the Zohar has cleverly hidden it in the confusion of color/Name/
radiance symbolism: Who are the "intelligent ones" of the verse in Daniel?
Look again at his definition. They are the mystics (one "who intuits on his
own things which one may not speak with the mouth"). And what sefirot
can the mystics "intuit"? If the verse is to be taken consistently, the
"intelligent ones" perceive ("shall be as radiant as") Tiferet (the radiant
firmament). We have, then, two very important points being made: (1) that
the mystics can perceive the sefirot; and (2) that they can "reach" even to
Tiferet, which is higher than the Patriarchs, and which is equal to the level
of Moses. These two points, especially the latter, are very radical, for they
imply that man still has direct revelatory contact with God, and that this
exists even on the level of Moses. Both implications contradict the
teachings of Rabbinic Judaism, which had asserted, as a matter of dogma,
that "prophecy" (i.e., direct revelatory contact) had ceased with the
Biblical period, and that Moses' prophecy was so superior that no one, not
even another Biblical prophet, could attain that level. Both of these dogmas
are here called into question. Note furthermore that just as the author of the
Zohar reinterpreted the term *creation* (to mean the flowing forth of the
sefirot and not the formation of the physical universe), so he here
reinterprets *prophecy/revelation* in mystical terms, taking it to mean the
mystical experience which the prophet undergoes by meditating on the

sefirot. This, too, is quite radical vis-à-vis the position of classical Judaism just noted.

Having expanded his use of verses (Exodus plus Daniel) and his use of symbol-set (colors/Names plus radiance/firmaments), and having added the mystic to those who are recipients of the direct contact with the divine (Patriarchs/Moses plus intelligent ones), the author of the Zohar, in the next section of this passage, expands his symbolism further with the imagery of colored lights, and he gives explicit instructions to the mystic.

> Come and see. There are four lights, three of them are hidden and one is revealed: the light which illumines, the light which is radiant and whose light is as the radiance of the heavens in their purity, the light of purple which gathers in all the [other] lights, and the light which does not illumine. [The last] looks to the others and gathers them in, and they are made visible in it as the reflector placed opposite the sun . . .
>
> The secret of this is [as follows]: Close your eyes and roll your pupils. Then, those colors which are luminous and radiant will be revealed. But permission is given to see them only with closed eyes, for they are the hidden, higher colors which are above those colors which are visible but nonradiant.

The four lights are, probably, as follows: Hokhma (the light which illumines), Bina (the light which is radiant), Tiferet (the purple light), and Maklhut (the light which does not illumine). It should be noted, however, that some interpreters take the four lights to be: Gevura, Hesed, Tiferet, and Malkhut. The former interpretation seems more consistent with the general symbolism of the Zohar. In any case, note that the last sefira acts only as a mirror or prism. Do not be confused by the fact that Hokhma is invisible in the color symbolism but illumines in the light symbolism. These are two separate symbol-sets which are artfully woven together in this passage.

The instructions to the mystic are very explicit. They are treated here as top-secret doctrine. The technique, however, is rather common in Eastern mysticism, and I have met students who are familiar with it. As mystical techniques go, it is not very sophisticated.

The author of the Zohar now introduces one last symbol-set into this passage, that of the luminous/nonluminous glass. It is based upon a passage in the Midrash which states that the other prophets saw God through a beclouded glass while Moses saw God through a luminous glass. (An alternate version understands the difference to be quantitative: nine glasses vs. one.) The luminous glass is Tiferet and the nonluminous glass is Malkhut. Having done this, the author of the Zohar then does his best to reassert the rabbinic dogma of the relative importance of the prophecy (i.e., the mystical experience) of Moses, the Patriarchs, and the mystic. According to the dogma, Moses must represent an unrepeatable rank, and hence the Patriarchs must be lower than Moses. The mystic, however, must also be heir to a direct and intense experience of the divine. Where does he stand?

> In this connection we read that Moses merited God [i.e., comprehended God] through the luminous glass which is placed above [the glass] which is nonluminous while the other people of this world [comprehend God only] through the nonluminous glass. The Patriarchs [however] comprehend the hidden [colors] which are above the nonluminous ones from those colors which were revealed. Therefore the verse says, "And I appeared to Abraham, to Isaac, and to Jacob [as] 'El Shaddai"—as those colors which are made manifest. "But [by] My Name, YHVH, I was not known to them"—these are the [still] higher, hidden, radiant [colors] which Moses merited to comprehend.
>
> And this is the secret: The eye can be open or closed. If it is closed, one sees the luminous glass. If it is open, one sees the nonluminous glass. Therefore the verse says "and I appeared," for of the nonluminous glass, which is of that which is manifest, [the word for] "seeing" is used, but of the luminous glass, which is of that which is hidden, [the word for] "knowing" is used. [At this] Rabbi Elazar and Rabbi Abba came and kissed the hands of Rabbi Shimon, and Rabbi Abba cried and said, "Woe when you depart from the world and it is orphaned of you. Who will be able to illumine the words of the Torah?" [II:23a–b]

This full, and complex, passage can now be summarized from several points of view. First, on the level of the sefirotic symbolism, we note that several symbol-systems have been interwoven. Thus, Tiferet is represented as YHVH (in the Name symbolism), as the radiant firmament (in the firmament symbolism), as the luminous glass (in the glass, or crystal, symbolism), as the purple light (in the light symbolism), and as containing the invisible and radiant colors (in the color symbolism). Malkhut is represented as El Shaddai, as the nonradiant firmament, as the nonluminous glass, as the nonilluminating light, and as containing the visible and nonradiant colors.

Second, from the viewpoint of the dogmatic concerns of the author of the Zohar, Tiferet is the level of Moses while Malkhut is the level of the Patriarchs. To this he adds that the word *knowing* is used of Tiferet (YHVH) in Exodus 6:3 while the word *appearing* is used of Malkhut (El Shaddai).

Third, in trying to place the mystic in the range of religious experience, the author of the Zohar starts with the assumption that prophecy-revelation must have been a type of mystical experience—i.e., that direct contact with the divine is a uniform event, that it is the same in all times and all places. Hence the prophets (Patriarchs included) were actually mystics, and hence their experience of God is not different from that of the Zoharic mystic. To place the mystic in this experiential continuum, the author of the Zohar asserts that the precedence of Moses over the Patriarchs is easily preserved. Moses perceived Tiferet, and the Patriarchs perceived Malkhut. The mystic, however, can perceive either Malkhut (the nonluminous glass) or Tiferet (the luminous glass), depending upon the technique he uses. The mystic can, thus, be of the level of the Patriarchs or of the level of Moses. This conclusion, however, conflicts with rabbinic dogma, which states that Moses must be in a nonrepeatable category. So the author of the Zohar left open a very clever solution. He appears to claim that Moses perceived Tiferet but also had an inkling of the more remote sefirot (the more hidden lights). This claim is not made for the mystic. The dogmatic and the experiential themes, thus, work themselves out as follows: The Patriarchs perceived Malkhut with an inkling of Tiferet. The mystic perceives Tiferet. Moses perceived Tiferet but with an inkling of the sefirot above it. The dogmatic order is preserved. The mystic is included in the class of individuals who achieve a genuine awareness of God. The verse in Exodus (which has given rise in modern times to the whole theory of Biblical higher criticism) is resolved. And all is accomplished with an artistic interweaving of symbol-systems into one dogmatic, experiential, and poetic whole.

On the fourth level of interpretation—the level of the meaning of the sefirotic symbolism—what has been said in this passage? First, we have been taught that religious experience is uniform in all ages. Prophecy and mysticism are one and the same because both are a contact between divine consciousness and human consciousness. Religious experience is a mixing of the divine and the human "image." It is concrete, real—as real as any other kind of experience, maybe more so. Second, we have been taught that for God, the mystical experience is a process of self-revelation. It is gradual but sure. At first He is hidden and luminous. Then He reveals part of Himself to the Patriarchs or the mystic—i.e., they, through meditation, may come to know Malkhut, which though nonluminous itself, nevertheless contains the reflection of the radiance and color of Tiferet. Finally, He reveals a more intimate aspect of Himself to Moses or to the mystic—i.e., they, through meditation, may come to know Tiferet, which is radiant of its own, and which for Moses reflects the radiance and color of His more hidden self.

What a stunning series of insights about God, and about the relationship between Him and man! For we are forced to reflect and consider: Is prophecy a *unilateral* choosing by God, a unilateral commissioning of an apostolic messenger? Or is prophecy a *mutual* finding of one another by God and man? Also, what is the mystical experience like from *God's* point of view? Is it a passive acceptance of the advances of the mystic, perhaps an uncaring and unconscious acceptance? Or is it really a self-revelation, a self-exposure of God's intimate being? Many stereotypic ideas in our general understanding of mysticism, as well as in our comprehension of Jewish tradition, are brought into question by reflecting upon this passage. Finally, we must reflect and consider: If mystical experience is a meeting of consciousnesses, and if that meeting is a mutual self-exposure, just what is the role of man in God's world? What function does man play in the progressive self-revelation of God? What role does man play in the intimate life of God? To this we must now turn.

9

THE ROLE OF MAN

Introduction

In the preceding chapter, we were introduced to the strange world of the Zohar. We have seen that, unlike the usual theologies and mystical treatises, the Zohar purports to speak of the inner being of God. It claims to speak not of His acts and words but of His consciousness. The Zohar purports to teach us something about the personality of God.

What have we learned about God's consciousness? The Zohar has taught us that God's being is His consciousness and that this consciousness is composed of ten elements called sefirot. Furthermore, the Zohar has taught us that God's consciousness is not a detached, impersonal consciousness floating in some ethereal, spiritual space. Rather it is a personalized, anthropopathic consciousness whose elements are vitally interactive. Thus, God is said to experience joy and despair, self-revelation and self-withdrawal, anger, power, grace, and balance. The Zohar has further taught that God's consciousness has inner and outer aspects, with the innermost aspects being unknowable in every sense of the word while the outermost aspects are His interface with the world. We have also seen that God's knowability is a function of the intelligence and intuition of the perceiver plus the self-definition of the Subject. The sequence of the self-articulation of God has also been spelled out together with the sequence of His self-revelation to man. And finally, we have been taught that God's personality can, ostensibly, be destabilized and restabilized by the actions of men.

In the area of the more usual theological concerns, we have learned that the Zohar has a definite theory of mystical experience. Something of the nature of that experience for man and the techniques needed to reach it have been expounded. Most startlingly, the nature of the mystical experience for God has also been shown. It is said to be an experience of intimate self-revelation to the mystic. The Zohar has also dealt with such dogmatic concerns as the relationship of prophecy to mysticism and, hence, the relative precedence of the prophets (particularly Moses) to the mystics. The reinterpretation of such traditional terms as *creation* and *revelation* has also been briefly expounded. Yet so much remains to be learned. The doctrine of the soul, the symbolism of the Tabernacle, and the nature of Torah, among many others, are unexplored themes. In English the Zohar occupies five volumes, and the selections given here are but a single breath taken in the breezes of a long spring. The interested reader must proceed further.

In matters of method, we have learned that reading the Zohar involves four levels of interpretation: identifying the Biblical "problem" that produces the Zoharic homily, understanding the general rabbinic interpretation of the passage, deciphering the sefirotic symbolism, and evaluating the meaning of that symbolism. Furthermore, the use of multiple symbol-systems to expound one idea has been amply demonstrated.

One major area of Zoharic thought deserves further exposition however, and it bases itself on an interesting question: If the personality of God is interactive, what is the role of man? Worded differently: If the consciousness of God is open to the consciousness of man, does man have a function in that relationship, and if so, what is it? We have seen that, apparently, God's personality can be destabilized and restabilized by man. How can that be done? Why would God so structure His own being as to be subject to the very power of man? What would the implications be for such ideas as sin, repentance, and messianism? To this we turn now. The first passage deals with the problem of the sin of Adam, and the last two passages deal with the Zoharic concept of prayer.

The Tree of Life and the Tree of the Knowledge of Good and Evil

This fascinating passage deals with three perennial questions. (1) The Genesis story indicates that there were two trees in the Garden of Eden: the Tree of Life, and the Tree of the Knowledge of Good and Evil. Are they one and the same, or different? (2) What was Adam's sin? Or, more properly, why did Adam sin? What motivated him to sin? (3) Why was the punishment of mortality meted out not only to man but to all living beings, for after all, animals are also mortal.

To understand the answers, one must decipher the sefirotic symbolism as follows: The Tree of Life is Tiferet, the Tree of the Knowledge of Good and Evil is Malkhut, and the Garden is the realm of the sefirot.

> Remark this: that God, when he made man and clothed him in great honor, made it incumbent that he cleave to him so as to be unique and of single heart, united to the One by the tie of the single-purposed faith which ties all together. And so it says: "And the Tree of Life was in the middle of the Garden" [Genesis 2:10]. But later, men abandoned the road of faith and left behind the singular tree which looms high over all trees, and adhered to the place which is continually shifting from one hue to another, from good to evil and evil to good, and they descended from on high and adhered below to the uncertain, and deserted the supreme and changeless One. Thus it was that their hearts, shifting between good and evil, caused them at times to merit mercy, at other punishment, depending on what it was that they had cleaved to.
>
> The Holy One, be blessed, spoke: Man, you have abandoned life and you cleave to death. "Life": this is the "Tree of Life" as it is written, "And the Tree of Life was in the midst of the Garden." It is called "Life" because one who holds on to it does not ever taste death. And you have clung to another tree; truly, death awaits you.—And so the decree was death, for him and for all the world.
>
> But if Adam transgressed, what was the sin of the rest of the world?

We know that all creatures did not come and eat of the forbidden tree, no. But it was this way: when man stood upright, all creatures, beholding him, were seized with fear of him, and slave-like they followed after him. And hence when he addressed them: "Come, let us bow down to the Lord who did make us" [Psalm 95:6]—they followed suit. But when they observed him making obeisance to the other place, adhering to it again, they did the same, and in this way did he bring about death for himself and all the world.

So did Adam move back and forth from one hue to another, from evil to good, from agitation to rest, from judgment to mercy, from life to death: never consistent in any one thing, because of the effect of that place, which is thus known as "the flaming sword which turned every way" [Genesis 3:24], from this direction to that from good to evil, from mercy to judgment, from peace to war. It [i.e., the sword] turns this way and that for every thing and it is called "good and evil" as it is written: "And from the Tree of the Knowledge of Good and Evil you shall not eat" [Genesis 2:17].

But the supreme King, out of compassion for his own handiworks, gave him warning, and said: "Of the tree of the knowledge of good and evil, thou shalt not eat of it" [Genesis 2:17]. Not heeding, man did as his wife, and was banished for ever, inasmuch as woman can come to this place, but not farther, and on her account death was decreed for all. But in time to come, "the days of my people shall be as the days of the tree" [Isaiah 65:22], like that singular tree we know of. Concerning that time it is written, "He will swallow up death for ever; and the Lord God will wipe away tears from all faces" [ibid. 25:8]. [III:107a–b]*

The answer to the first question, then, is as follows: The Tree of Life is not the same as the Tree of the Knowledge of Good and Evil. The former is constant, unified, having no internal split or dichotomy. In the sefirotic world of discourse, Tiferet, which is the center of God's personality, is unity. To reach the level of meditating on Tiferet is to experience the transcendent unity of the divine. Malkhut, on the other hand, is the confluence of all the conflicting elements, and hence contains within itself conflict and contradiction. It turns over and over; it changes its hues. One side of its nature is severity, war, evil, and death. To meditate on Malkhut is to experience the governance of the cosmos, the point where the divine, in all its multifacetedness, must touch and act upon the nondivine.

The answer to the second question is as follows: Adam sat in the Garden, i.e., he meditated upon the sefirot. He saw unchanging Tiferet and changing Malkhut, and he was drawn to the latter. God warned him not to meditate

---

*Trans. G. Scholem, *Zohar*, pp. 119–20.

on Malkhut, but he, following his wife, did so anyway. His sin consisted, first, in defying God's warning. But, as we have seen, he appears to have been distracted by Malkhut even before God issued His warning. So Adam's sin, in a more profound sense, is independent of Eve and consisted in letting himself be distracted from divine unity and simplicity to divine plurality and complexity. Adam preferred the enigmas of providential action to the tranquility of transcendent unity. He chose the wrong side of God; he allowed a split in the divine. Why was Adam attracted to Malkhut? This text does not say. Is it because, being less than divine, he preferred multiplicity to unity? Is it because providence is truly a manifestation of divine power, and Adam, the nondivine being, wanted to have that divine power?

Reflecting upon the fact that it may well be man's will to divine power (and not to divine unity) that motivates man, we can understand why meditating on Malkhut alone became the sin *par excellence* in the Zohar, for to be content with puzzling over the vagaries of God's providence is to be distracted by only one aspect of His being. To continually confront the question of the Holocaust as a problem in theodicy (the justice of God's providential action), for example, is to recommit Adam's sin, that is, to allow a split in the divine. "Sin"—every man's sin—is becoming preoccupied with one aspect of God. "Idolatry" is worshipping (meditating on) only one aspect of the totality that is God. And, conversely, "redemption" (as we shall see) is "unifying" all God's aspects. "Worship" is a meditative fusing of divine diversity into divine simplicity. It also follows from this that, in the "end of days," when the sin of Adam will have been reversed by a change in the nature of man due to the coming of the Messiah, man's meditation will again be on the Tree of Life (Tiferet), and hence mortality will be abolished, as predicted by Isaiah. Note, incidentally, that the text says clearly that women, in meditation, cannot reach beyond Malkhut. It is a given; no explanation is offered. As to the animals: Before the sin, they were intelligent beings. They too could meditate, though not as fully as man. They follow man in meditation. When man becomes distracted, so do those who follow him. The animals, too, chose divine plurality and power over divine simplicity and unity. Therefore, they too are mortal.

The Meaning of the Minyan

Commentary by K. Kogan

The Zoharic attitude toward prayer, in line with mystical thought in general, regards man's actions and thoughts during worship as having additional significance above and beyond that ascribed to them by rabbinic tradition. Prayer was regarded by the Kabbalists as having an influence on mundane existence only secondarily, through its effects upon the heavenly realm of divine emanations—the world of the sefirot. In the conscious or unconscious attempt to appear as remaining within the tradition, however, the authors of the early mystical texts refrained from rewriting the liturgy in terms of the new conception, confining their innovation to a reinterpretation of traditional prayers and practices. The Zoharic passage interpreted here is illustrative of this reinterpretation process.

> R. Eleazar began a discourse on the verse: "Wherefore, when I came, was there no man?" etc. (Isaiah 50:2). How beloved, he said, are Israel before the Holy One, blessed be He, in that wherever they dwell He is found among them, for He never withdraws His mercy from them. We find it written: "And let them make Me a sanctuary, that I may dwell among them" (Exodus 25:8), that is, any sanctuary whatever, inasmuch as any synagogue, wherever situated, is called sanctuary. And the Shekinah hastens to the synagogue (before the worshipers). Worthy is the man who is of the first ten to enter synagogue, since they form something complete, and are the first to be sanctified by the Shekinah.

This first section is essentially a restatement of the traditional conception of the *minyan*. The verse from Isaiah is traditionally associated with the requirement of the ten-man quorum, and the idea that God is present in some form at such a gathering is not new. In the last sentence quoted, however, the phrase "something complete" refers to more than simply the completed quorum. The ten men symbolize the complete heavenly realm of ten sefirot, which also makes up the body of the Adam Kadmon (primordial man), as will be seen in the next section. Therefore, within the passage it is considered admirable to be of the first ten to enter the synagogue not only because this number fulfills the quorum, but also because one is then a part

146

of the symbolic replica of the sefirotic realm, of the Spiritual Adam. It is this symbolic construct that is sanctified.

> But it is necessary that the ten should come together at the same time and not in sections, so as not to delay the completion of the body in its members. So did the Holy One, blessed be He, make man all at one time, and establish all his members in one act. So we read: "Hath he not made thee and established thee?" (Deuteronomy 32:6). [Just as man had all limbs completed at once, therefore when the Shekinah comes early to synagogue, it is necessary that ten people be found there as one and everything is created. Afterwards, everything else comes into place.] Those that come later are the mere "adornments of the body."

That the ten men must come together at the same time is an additional requirement, and is (as far as practical ordinances go) the main point of the entire passage. The reason for this ruling hinges upon the mystical conception of the *minyan* as symbolizing the sefirotic realm, and further, upon the idea that the sefirot taken together make up some sort of body. If the author were considering the ten men to be simply the fulfillment of a quorum, it would not matter whether they came all at once or individually. He is pointing out, however, that this group symbolizes the body of the Adam Kadmon, and therefore that it is wrong for it to be formed in sections.

The statement that the remaining members of the congregation are mere adornments of the body underlines the special function and importance of the initial ten. This special function is further clarified in the following section of the passage:

> But when the people do not arrive together the Holy One, blessed be He, exclaims: "Why do I come and there is no man?" For inasmuch as the single members are not together there is no complete body, and so that is "no man." Observe that the moment the body is made complete here below a supernal holiness comes and enters that body, and so the lower world is in truth transformed after the pattern of the upper world.

On one level, the body that is formed below, the actual *minyan,* is entered by the Shekhina (the supernal holiness), and is thus the point of contact between God and Israel. Simultaneously, the *minyan* formed in the proper manner below unifies the heavenly realm above, preparing it for union between the Shekhima (Malkhut) and Tiferet. When the *minyan* is formed, the Shekhina comes to dwell within it on earth, and at the same time (by virtue of the *minyan*'s symbolic action) she is in union with Tiferet in the sefirotic realm. That the lower world is transformed after the manner of the upper world refers to this parallel union as well as to the replication of the ten sefirot by the group of ten men. The practical ramifications of all this divine activity are summed up in the final section of the passage:

> Thus it is incumbent on all not to open their mouths to talk of worldly matters, seeing that Israel then are at their most complete and holiest. Happy is their portion! [III:126a]*

The entire passage, then, consists of a statement about the proper formation of the *minyan* followed by an explanation of the importance of this particular ritual in terms of the supernal drama it inspires. A further ordinance against worldly chatter during the drama follows, and the passage closes with a note of satisfaction about Israel's importance that is an appropriate and logical conclusion to such an explanation of the divine significance of Israel's actions.

---

*Trans. H. Sperling and J. Abelson, *The Zohar* (London: Soncino Press, 1934), 5:184–85.

Sacrifice and the Heavenly Union
Commentary by K. Kogan

In this passage the author of the Zohar sets forth his conception of prayer. The opening section deals specifically with the issue of praise before prayer, in the traditional sense. (In the traditional liturgy, a series of Psalms of praise precedes the petitional Silent Prayer—Ed.)

R. Jose and R. Hizkiah were once going to see R. Simeon in Cappadocia. Said R. Hizkiah: We have laid down that a man before praying should first pronounce God's praises. But what of the man who is in great distress and is in haste to pour out his prayer and is not able to pronounce the blessings of his Master fittingly? He replied: That is no reason why the praise of his Master should be omitted. He should pronounce it, even without proper devotion, and then say his prayer. Thus it is written: "A prayer of David, hear, O Lord, righteousness, listen to my song" (Psalm 17:1)—first praise and then prayer. Of him who is able to pronounce the praise of his Master and does not do so, it is written: "Yea, when ye make many prayers I will not hear" (Isaiah 61:15).

In this section the author simply states that praise must precede prayer even if the praise is not uttered with proper intention. Here, greater importance is ascribed to the ritual of the liturgy than to the momentary state of mind of the worshiper. The following section is, however, more specifically theosophical.

It is written: "The one lamb thou shalt offer in the morning, and the second lamb shalt thou offer at even" (Numbers 8:4). Prayers have been ordained to correspond to the daily offerings. Through the impulse from below there is a stirring above, and through the impulse from above there is a stirring higher up still, until the impulse reaches the place where the lamp is to be lit and it is lit. Thus, by the impulse of

149

the smoke (of the sacrifice) from below, the lamp is kindled above, and when this is kindled all the other lamps are kindled and all the worlds are blessed from it. Thus the impulse of the sacrifice is the rehabilitation [*tikkun*] of the world and the blessing of all worlds.

In this section, the Talmudic parallel between prayer and sacrifice is cited, and it provides a foundation for the ensuing description of the heavenly workings of man's impulse to worship. The explanation given as applying to sacrifice is later applied to prayer by means of this parallel.

The rest of this section outlines the mystical interpretation of the effect of sacrifice upon the divine realm. The "impulse from below" refers, on one level, to man's general desire to worship, and the physical action of sacrifice that follows from that desire. On another level, this "impulse" refers to the specific mystical intention of the worshiper during the act of worship. What this specific intention must be becomes clear as the passage progresses, for it involves a concentration upon the divine events as described later in the passage.

The "impulse from below" is, then, described as ascending into the heavenly realm, creating a "stirring above." This "stirring above" is (or produces) the "impulse from above," which is the desire of Malkhut, the female element, to unite with Tiferet, the male element. The "impulse from above" produces a "stirring higher up still," which is the impulse of Tiferet to descend and to unite with Malkhut. The "place where the lamp is to be lit" may be Tiferet, or even Binah. Thus, the "impulse from below"— man's impulse—sets in motion impulses and stirrings in the divine realm, which, in turn, set in motion the flow of blessings and rehabilitate the order and unity of the divine realm. The passage continues in greater detail.

When the smoke commences to rise, the holy forms in charge of the world derive satisfaction, and are disposed thereby to stir the grades above them; and so the impulse rises until the King desires to associate with the Matron. Through the yearning of the lower world, the lower waters flow forth to meet the upper waters, for the upper waters do not flow save from the impulse of the desire from below. Thus, mutual desire in kindled and the lower waters flow to meet the upper waters, and worlds are blessed, and all lamps are kindled, and upper and lower [realms] are endowed with blessing.

The process of prayer, then, is as follows: The first level of divine life, the angels, is here described as "the holy forms in charge of the world." The impulse of worship pleases them, and moves them to pass on the "message" to the sefirot, specifically Tiferet (King) and Malkhut (Matron). When the impulse reaches Tiferet, it instills in him a desire to have sexual union with the Shekhina (Malkhut). Simultaneously, the Shekhina is inspired by the impulse to be united with Tiferet and moves upwards to meet him. This is what is meant by the lower waters (Shekhina) flowing to meet the upper waters (Tiferet). "The upper waters flowing only in response to desire from below" is a symbol with multiple meanings. It refers to the actual movement of Tiferet in the direction of Malkhut, to his emotional desire to be united with her, and also to the blessings which he has the power to release. The "desire from below" which inspires Tiferet comes both from Israel's worship on earth and from the desire of the Shekhina, who has also been inspired by Israel's sacrifice. That this desire is mutual—on the part of Tiferet and Malkhut—is stressed as being the ingredient required for a union between the two such that the flow of blessings (here symbolized by the light) will result.

That both upper and lower worlds are endowed with blessings indicates that the heavenly realm is, in some sense, in need of these blessings, and therefore that Israel's impulse during worship is of benefit to God.

> Observe that the function of the priests and levites is to unite the Left with the Right. Said R. Hizkiah: That is so, but I have been told that one rouses the Left and the other the Right, because the union of male and female is only brought about by Left and Right, as it says: "O that his left hand were under my head, and his right hand should embrace me" (Song of Songs 2:6).

In this section the role of several other sefirot in the heavenly union is brought into focus. The "Left" and "Right" refer to the left and the right sides of the sefirotic realm: The Left (Gevura, and Hod) represents God's stern, judgmental aspects, and the Right, (Hesed and Nesah) represents the loving, merciful tendencies of God.

The inclusion of the passage from the Song of Songs implies that the left and right sides of the sefirotic realm each play a specific role in the heavenly union of Tiferet with Malkhut. This speculation is strengthened by the mystical interpretation of the traditional functions of the priests and levites. The priests, by virtue of their sacrificial appeasement of God's stern "side," rouse His right (loving) side, while the levites rouse the judgmental, left side. The exact functions of the two sides in the heavenly union is not clear from this passage, but it is evident that both are important in bringing about the union. The point of this section is to impress upon the reader the importance of including in his meditations specific attention to both the harsh and the merciful aspects of God.

> Then male and female are united and there is mutual desire and worlds are blessed, and upper and lower rejoice. Hence we see that sacrifice is

the support and the rehabilitation of the world, and the joy of the upper and lower [realms].

This section summarizes the outcome of the impulse of sacrifice: that it leads (by the process described above) to union within God (portrayed in a sexual image), the products of which are a flow of blessings for both man and the divine realm, and joy for man and God. The assertion that "sacrifice is the support of the world" leads one to believe that, according to the author, blessings from God can flow down to earth *only* as a result of Israel's religious activity. That Israel, therefore, is of vital importance to the harmonious existence of all life on earth is a logical conclusion, and a statement to this effect concludes the passage.

> Said R. Jose: You are certainly right, and I had heard this before but had forgotten it. This, too, I have learnt, that nowadays prayer takes the place of sacrifice, and a man should fittingly pronounce the praise of his Master, and if not, his prayer is no prayer. The most perfect form of praising God is to unify the Holy Name in the fitting manner for, through this, upper and lower are set in motion, and blessings flow to all worlds.

The statement that prayer now takes the place of sacrifice serves to apply the entire preceding explanation to prayer. The ritual that links prayer to sacrifice—the obligatory inclusion of praise—is then given a mystical interpretation. Clearly implied is that prayer must be recited with proper intention—that is, with mental concentration upon its influence in the realm of the sefirot. In fact, much of the significance of this passage as a whole lies in the fact that it sets a new ideal for *Kavvana*. Proper devotion here becomes a kind of meditation with semi-magical intent. One's concentration on the activities of the sefirot during prayer transforms worship from a simple expression of need or emotion to an almost magical activity. The magical technique does not involve the use of special phrases or actions, but rather the more subtle tool of mental intent. It is clearly implied in the passage that God's control over the world is monitored not by His own will, but by His "emotional" reactions to the nuances of intention underlying Israel's prayers.

The final statement,

> R. Hizkiah said: God placed Israel in exile among the nations in order that they might be blessed for their sake, for they do bring blessings from heaven to earth every day. [I:243b—244a]*

---

*Trans. H. Sperling and I. Abelson, *The Zohar*, 2:374–75.

seems to be the climax of the passage. The dramatic influence of Israel's prayer upon the divine realm, culminating in a flow of blessings for heaven and the world, is strong support indeed for the belief that Israel's exile is for a purpose, and that Israel performs a vital function in Creation.

(Editor's note: The importance of the twice-daily sacrifice, and of the subsequent substitution of liturgical prayer, lay in the fact that the sacrificial lamb atoned for the sins of the world and thus allowed God to maintain His creation. The Christian reader will immediately recognize the *Agnus Dei qui tollit peccata mundi,* and should note that the parallel is to the daily, and not to the Paschal, sacrifice.)

Conclusion

Just as the Zohar represents a radical shift in our thinking about God, so it represents a radical shift in our thinking about man. For according to the Zohar, God's relationship with the world is patterned on the model of a continuous flow of energy. God generates the energy, but it is man who must act like a prism, focusing and returning the energy to God. This energy, then, is renewed and returned to man, who again focuses and returns it to God, and so on. In the language of very contemporary man, the relationship of God's energy to the world is one of recycling: God generates, man recycles. It is a continuous process. It is elliptical in form, having two foci. God does not act independently of man. He does not act unilaterally. God and man stand in a reciprocal relationship, each benefiting the other, each doing something that allows the other to achieve full existence. The image of man as the prism (recycling agent) of the divine energy is crucial to the Zohar, and it is, in the Jewish mystical tradition, a new idea.

How was this refocusing (recycling) effect accomplished? As we have seen, the twice-daily offering prescribed in Numbers 8:4 was the basic sacrifice of the Temple service. It was offered every day, even on the most important holidays. The reason for this was that this sacrifice atoned for the sins of the world, and hence it was the act which allowed God to maintain the universe in existence. When the sacrificial cult was abolished because of the destruction of the Temple, liturgical prayer took the place of sacrifice. This ritual prayer was also recited twice daily (later, thrice), and it too became the act which appeased God and which, therefore, sustained the world. In Rabbinic Judaism, however, these associations were not made explicit. Prayer, especially ritual prayer, remained one of many commandments of the Torah, as interpreted by the rabbis, which one had to fulfill. The author of the Zohar, in adding a new dimension to ritualized prayer, brought it back very close to the original intent of the sacrifices, for prayer again became an act which corrected the sins of the world and opened up the flow of divine energy. How was this to be done?

Rabbinic Judaism had already developed the technique known as *Kavvana*, which was intended to accompany the recitation of the liturgy. This technique, coming from the root meaning "to direct the heart (consciousness)," allowed the practicing rabbinic Jew to focus his attention not only on the words and their meanings but also upon a host of other things. He might bring into his awareness a consciousness of other Jews in other places and times. It is not unusual, for example, for the praying rabbinic Jew of today to call to mind, during his prayers, the Six Million who died at the hands of the Nazis. (How *did* they pray?) The praying Jew might bring into his awareness a consciousness of the power of God or His justice. He might also focus upon the personal Presence of God, and so on. This technique of *Kavvana*, then, was (and is) a consciousness-raising technique, allowing one who practices it to focus (direct) his consciousness to one or several things while, at the same time, reciting the liturgical texts. The technique was known to every rabbinic Jew. It may have been formally studied when the relevant sections of the law were studied. It was certainly learned from observing people praying and from reading the pietistic literature.

To this basic consciousness-directing technique called *Kavvana*, the author of the Zohar added a new dimension—concentration upon the activity of the various sefirot. The Jewish mystic who adopted the Zoharic view of the world would, thus, have to hold in his (I doubt that any women practiced this type of meditation) consciousness the liturgy and the usual rabbinic associations, and at the same time, he would have to be conscious of the divine flow of energy coming from, and within, the realm of the sefirot. He would have to be able not only to sense this flow but to focus it, to redirect it, back to its source. The flow would, then, come down to him and be returned by him to the realms of the angels and then to the realm of the sefirot. He would attempt to motivate Malkhut (God's Face to the World; His outer self) to reunite with Tiferet (God's balanced, inner self). He would attempt to call down Gevura (God's justice, even His anger) and Hesed (God's grace, His unconditional love) and to fuse them into Tiferet and into the subsequent union between Tiferet and Malkhut. In a word, the worshiper would, by focusing the flow of divine energy, try to restore an inner harmony within God. He would try to achieve a unity among God's varying characteristics. He would seek to achieve an inner peace for God. In so doing, the flow of energy would be restored to its higher sources (Bina, Hokhma, and Keter), and having touched home (so to speak), the energy would be able to flow freely down the ontological ladder, back toward man and the world. This process was called *Tikkun*, the rehabilitation of God and reality.

To the traditional rabbinic Jew, all this was (and is) very strange. Yet we have even stranger sections of the Zohar, which speak of the divine channels being blocked, i.e., of something having happened within God that prevents, or obstructs, the flow of divine energy. And then it is man who must come along and, through Zoharic *Kavvana* (i.e., through focusing the energy flow), release the obstructions. It is man who must help to restore the divine flow when it is stopped. It is man who must restore, or "rehabilitate," God.

We are now in a position to appreciate more fully the nature of sin in the Zohar, for sin, as we have seen, is actually the misfocusing of the divine energy. It is man's distraction and subsequent misdirection of the divine light. The reason is now clear: Man acts like a prism, for better *and* for worse. Man recycles, for better *and* for worse. Sin, whether it be Adam's paradigmatic sin or that of any person, is thus a misuse of divine energy. Furthermore, this misuse still contains power. It is, after all, divine energy, even if it is misfocused. Sin, therefore, is also that which causes blockages and imbalances in the divine flow. Sin is that which creates impedances and resistances to the harmonious, balanced flow of divine energy. Experienced evil, therefore, is the result of this imperfect, unbalanced flow of the divine energy. In a word, sin destabilizes God while proper prayer restabilizes Him.

If we consider these insights on the fourth level of interpretation (the level of meaning and implication), we should note, first, that the concepts of "sin" and "prayer" (like the concepts of "creation" and "revelation") have undergone a vast change. Prayer is no longer praise and petition with an expanded awareness of the power and Presence of God. Prayer has developed into a kind of theurgy, a kind of psychotherapy that man works upon God. For we are able, according to the Zohar, by our own sensing and focusing of the divine energy, to reach into God and help Him straighten Himself out, to help Him restore His own inner peace and balance. We are also able, according to the Zohar, to disrupt the flow of God's being. Seen from God's point of view, God is, according to the Zohar, inherently given to moments of instability, and He needs man in order to maintain His own balance. He thus can be hurt, even crippled, by man, and He can be helped, even sustained, by him.

We should also note that we have before us a very powerful, and in some ways new, insight into the nature of the man-God relationship, for the Zohar is teaching us that God is actually dependent upon man. The Zohar teaches that God, having committed Himself to creation, now needs it. This insight is heretical and orthodox at one and the same time. It is orthodox because rabbinic Judaism had always taught that man was the partner of God, that God's actions were in large measure a response to man's obedience and disobedience. The author of the Zohar has simply taken this insight a little further and applied it to the inner workings of God. The insight is heretical because it forces us to ask the question: What happened to God's omnipotence? Is He all-powerful? The Zoharic answer is no.

We should also note that this insight into God's basic dependence upon man is, actually, frightening, because more than ever before in Jewish thought, man is the active agent. It is man who is responsible for the balance of forces in God. It is man who is responsible for the flow of divine energy in God and in the world. It is man who is responsible not only for his own mental health but for God's as well. As God becomes more dependent upon man, man becomes more responsible. As God grants man more power, not only over the world but over Himself, man must face the responsibility that goes with that power.

The concerned reader will, at this point, wish to reflect honestly on several questions: Aside from the difficulty that the modern person has in accepting realms of sefirot, etc., would you want to have a God Who is dependent upon mankind? Would you really want to have a God Whose consciousness mixes with humankind's in a reciprocal relationship? Or does that definition of God somehow seem un-Godly? Why? And yet, which conception is more realistic? more spiritual? even, more humanistic? Which is "better"? It is strange to note that, although the Zohar was written about 1290 C.E., mankind still seems unwilling to face up to the responsibility of helping to rule the universe. Jewish mystical tradition, far from fleeing from this responsibility, developed theories which intensified it and which specified how one is to "go in unto" God. Later Zoharic tradition increased, not decreased, the importance of man in the divine scheme of things. And to this we turn next.

10

THE LURIANIC DEVELOPMENT

Introduction

The world of zoharic thought was a very rich world. It contained many new and startling ideas, but these very ideas allowed the intelligent reader to again strike up a personal relationship with God. Through the Zohar, the learned and spiritually sensitive Jew could once more probe deeply into the interpersonal nature of the man-God relationship. This personalism had been one of the core ideas of Biblical Judaism. It had been one of the core ideas of Rabbinic Judaism. It had, however, been glossed over by the philosophical and legalistic developments of Rabbinic Judaism. And suddenly it was available again, and with an intense mystical praxis accompanying it too.

The Zohar had, nonetheless, left open several questions. (1) If God, before beginning the process of His own self-articulation, was alone, occupying all nonspace and nontime, where did He begin to articulate Himself? Or, worded differently: Even the sefirot exist in some realm of transcendental space-time. Where is that realm? Did God not first have to create such a realm in order to be able to make room for His own self-articulation? (2) Was the process of the emanation of the sefirot (the process of the self-articulation of God) as smooth as the metaphors of the flowing stream and emanating light suggest? Or were there conflicts in the very process of self-definition in God Himself, conflicts of shatteringly powerful proportions? And (3), in the Zohar, man is to act as the prism of the divine light (as the recycler of the divine energy), but is the process really so simple? Or was the self-articulation of God so shattering that man must scamper to pick up the pieces? Is man a turnaround point or is man really in the position of the king's men who tried to put Humpty-Dumpty back together again?

About 250 years after the writing of the Zohar, a new teacher arose who tried to answer some of these questions. Rabbi Isaac Luria, who lived in the generation after the expulsion of the Jews from the Iberian Peninsula, dwelt in the Holy Land in the city of Safed and lived among some of the most powerful mystics and legalists in Jewish history. His works have not come down to us, but those of two of his students are available. These treatises are very, very complex, and I have had to content myself with G. Scholem's lucid summary of the Lurianic myth presented in the following selection. The reader will want to do three things: First, it is necessary to identify as clearly as possible the three great moments in the Lurianic myth: *tsimtsum* (the self-limitation of God), *shevirah* (the shattering of the vessels), and *tikkun* (the restoration of the cosmos and God to the primordial unity). Be sure to note how this last moment is accomplished. Second, the reader will want to identify the following terms and their role in the Lurianic myth: *tehiru* (the pneumatic, primordial space), *partsufim* (the configurations of the sefirot), the "four worlds" (Emanation, Creation, Formation, and Making), *kelippot* (the shells, the demonic), and the "sparks" (the remnants of the divine light). Finally, the reader will want to ask: What is the nature of prayer in this system? What are the messianic implications of the system? And why does Scholem call this a "myth of exile and redemption"? The material is complex, but a careful reading of it will yield the necessary answers.

The Lurianic Myth

by G. Scholem*

In the foregoing we have discussed a few Kabbalistic symbols, which, it seems to me, excellently illustrate the nature of the problem of Kabbalah and myth. But in the systems of the early Kabbalists, and particularly of the *Zohar,* we find not only a revival of isolated mythical motifs, but also a dense texture of mythical ideas often constituting fully developed myths. Many of the Kabbalists, as we have seen, busied themselves with the speculative and theological reinterpretation of such mythical thinking. But interesting as such reinterpretation may be from the standpoint of the history of ideas, it cannot blind us to the psychic substance underlying the myths. In many cases, I am almost inclined to think, the speculative reformulation of myths was quite secondary even in the minds of those who engaged in it and served merely as an exoteric disguise for the mythical content which they looked upon as a holy mystery.

Apart from the *Zohar,* myth is exemplified most strikingly and magnificently in the most important system of the late Kabbalah, the system of Isaac Luria (1534–72) of Safed, and later in the heretical *theologoumena* of the Sabbatians, whose Kabbalistic Messianism was in part inspired by Luria. Both the orthodox Kabbalah of Luria and the heretical Kabbalah of Nathan of Gaza (1644–80), prophet and theologian of Sabbatai Zevi, the Kabbalistic Messiah, provide amazingly complete examples of gnostic myth formation within or on the fringe of Rabbinical Judaism. The one is a strictly orthodox form of such gnosis, the other a heretical, antinomian deviation. Both forms of Kabbalistic myth are closely related to the historical experience of the Jewish people, and this no doubt accounts in large part for the fascination which both, but especially the Lurianic Kabbalah, have undoubtedly exerted on large sections of the Jewish people, namely, those whose keen religious sensibility prepared them to

---

From G. Scholem, *On the Kabbalah and Its Symbolism* (New York: Schocken Books, 1965), pp. 109–17.

play a leading role in the religious development. Here I cannot enter into the heretical mythology of the Sabbatians; but I should like to describe, at least in its broad outlines, the structure of Lurianic myth as an unparalleled example of the contexts with which we are here concerned. It may seem presumptuous to attempt such a summary of a body of thought which in its canonical literary form fills several thick volumes, especially as much of it can be fathomed only in the practice of mystical meditation and, as far as I can see, defies theoretical formulation. And yet the underlying structure, Luria's fundamental myth, is so amazingly clear that even a brief analysis of it should prove fruitful.

From a historical point of view, Luria's myth constitutes a response to the expulsion of the Jews from Spain, an event which more than any other in Jewish history down to the catastrophe of our time gave urgency to the question: why the exile of the Jews and what is their vocation in the world? This question, the question of the meaning of the Jews' historical experience in exile, is here dealt with even more deeply and fundamentally than in the *Zohar;* it lies indeed at the heart of the new conceptions which are the essence of Luria's system.

Luria's new myth is concentrated in three great symbols, the *tsimtsum,* or self-limitation, of God, the *shevirah,* or breaking of the vessels, and the *tikkun,* or harmonious correction and mending of the flaw which came into the world through the *shevirah.*

The *tsimtsum* does not occur in the *Zohar.* It originates in other old treatises, but became truly significant only with Luria. It is an amazing conception. The *tsimtsum* ushers in the cosmic drama. But this drama is no longer, as in older systems, an emanation or projection, in which God steps out of Himself, communicates or reveals Himself. On the contrary, it is a withdrawal into Himself. Instead of turning outward, He contracts His essence, which becomes more and more hidden. Without the *tsimtsum* there would be no cosmic process, for it is God's withdrawal into Himself that first creates a pneumatic, primordial space—which the Kabbalists called *tehiru*—and makes possible the existence of something other than God and His pure essence. The Kabbalists do not say so directly, but it is implicit in their symbolism that this withdrawal of the divine essence into itself is a primordial exile, or self-banishment. In the *tsimtsum* the powers of judgment, which in God's essence were united in infinite harmony with the "roots" of all other potencies, are gathered and concentrated in a single point, namely, the primordial space, or pleroma, from which God withdraws. But the powers of stern judgment ultimately include evil. Thus the whole ensuing process, in which these powers of judgment are eliminated from, or "smelted out" of, God, is a gradual purification of the divine organism from the elements of evil. This doctrine, which definitely conflicts with other themes in Luria's own system and is more than questionable from a theological point of view, is consistently attenuated or disregarded in most expositions of the Lurianic system. In the *Tree of Life,* the great work of Luria's disciple Hayim Vital, the *tsimtsum* becomes, not a necessary and fundamental crisis in God Himself, but a free act of love, which however, paradoxically enough, first unleashes the powers of stern judgment.

In the primordial space, or pleroma, the "roots of judgment" discharged in the *tsimtsum* are mixed with the residue of God's infinite light, which has withdrawn from it. The nature of the forms that come into being in the pleroma is determined by the cooperation and conflict between these two elements and by the workings of a third element, a ray from God's essence, which subsequently breaks through and falls back into the primordial space. For Luria, the events that take place in the pleroma are intradivine. It is these manifestations of the infinite in the pleroma which for Luria constitute the one living God. He tries to describe the genesis of these manifestations. For the part of God which has not entered into the process of *tsimtsum* and the following stages, His infinite essence, that remains hidden, is often of little importance to man here below. The conflict between the personal character of God even before the *tsimtsum* and His true impersonal essence, which takes on personality only with the process begun in the *tsimtsum,* remains unresolved in the classical forms of the Lurianic myth.

In the pleroma arise the archetypes of all being, the forms, determined by the structure of the *sefiroth,* of *Adam Kadmon,* of the creator God who takes a hand in Creation. But the precarious co-existence of the different kinds of divine light produces new crises. Everything that comes into being after the ray of the light from *en-sof* has been sent out into the pleroma is affected by the twofold movement of the perpetually renewed *tsimtsum* and of the outward flowing emanation. Every stage of being is grounded in this tension. From the ears, the mouth, and the nose of the Primordial Man burst forth lights which produce deeply hidden configurations, states of being and inner worlds beyond the penetration of the human mind, even in meditation. But the central plan of Creation originates in the lights which shine in strange refraction from the eyes of *Adam Kadmon.* For the vessels which, themselves consisting of lower mixtures of light, were designed to receive this mighty light of the *sefiroth* from his eyes and so to serve as vessels and instruments of Creation, shattered under its impact. This is the decisive crisis of all divine and created being, the "breaking of the vessels," which Luria identifies with the Zoharic image of the "dying of the primordial kings." For the *Zohar* interprets the list of the kings of Edom in Genesis 36, who reigned and died "before there were kings in Israel," as an allusion to the pre-existence of worlds of stern judgment, which were destroyed by the excess of this element within them. In Luria the death of the kings from lack of harmony between the masculine and feminine elements, described in the *Zohar,* is transformed into the "breaking of the vessels," also a crisis of the powers of judgment, the most unassimilable parts of which are projected downward in this cataclysm to lead an existence of their own as demonic powers. Two hundred and eighty-eight sparks from the fire of "judgment," the hardest and the heaviest, fall, mingling with the fragments of the broken vessels. For after the crisis nothing remains as it was. All the lights from the eyes of *Adam Kadmon* return upward, rebounding from the vessels, or break through downward. Luria describes the laws governing this event in detail. Nothing remains in its proper place. Everything is somewhere else. But a being that is not in its proper place is in exile. Thus, since that primordial act, all being has been a being in exile, in need of being led back and redeemed. The breaking of the vessels continues into all the further stages of emanation and Creation; everything is in some way broken, everything has a flaw, everything is unfinished.

But what was the reason for this cleavage in God? This question was bound to arise in the Lurianic Kabbalah, though a definitive solution was never arrived at. The esoteric answer, which puts it down as a purification of God himself, a necessary crisis, whose purpose it was to eliminate evil from God, undoubtedly reflects Luria's own opinion but, as we have seen, it was seldom stated openly—an exception is Joseph ibn Tabul, Luria's second important disciple. Others content themselves with the time-honoured allusion to the law of the organism, to the image of the seed that bursts and dies in order to become wheat. The powers of judgment are likened to seeds of grain which are sowed in the field of the *tehiru* and sprout in Creation, but only in the metamorphosis they undergo through the breaking of the vessels and the death of the primordial kings.

Thus the original crisis, which in gnostic thinking is fundamental to an understanding of the drama and secret of the cosmos, becomes an element in the experience of exile. As an experience affecting God Himself, or at least in the manifestation of His essence, exile takes on the enormous dimensions which it had obviously assumed for the Jews of those generations. It was the very boldness of this gnostic paradox—exile as an element in God Himself—that accounted in large part for the enormous influence of these ideas among the Jews. Before the judgment seat of rationalist theology such an idea may not have much to say for itself. But for the human experience of the Jews it was the most powerful and seductively appropriate of symbols.

And so the vessels of the *sefiroth,* which were to receive the world emanating from *Adam Kadmon,* are broken. In order to mend this breach or restore the edifice which, now that the demonized powers of pure judgment have been eliminated, would seem to be capable of taking on a harmonious and definitive form, healing, constructive lights have issued from the forehead of *Adam Kadmon*. Their influence ushers in the third stage in the symbolic process, which the Kabbalists called *tikkun*, restoration. For Luria this process takes place partly in God, but partly in man as the crown of all created being. It is an intricate process, for though the powers of evil were cast out in the breaking of the vessels, they were not wholly eliminated. The process of elimination must continue, for the configurations of the *sefiroth* that now arise still contain vestiges of the pure power of judgment, and these must either be eliminated or transformed into constructive powers of love and mercy. In five figures, or configurations, which Luria calls *partsufim*, "faces" of God or of *Adam Kadmon*, Primordial Man is reconstructed in the world of *tikkun*. These fives faces are *'arikh*, "Long-suffering"; the Father; the Mother; the *ze'ir 'anpin*, "Impatient"; and his feminine complement, the *Shekhinah*, who in turn is manifested in two configurations, Rachel and Leah. Everything that the *Zohar* had to say about the *conjunctio* of the masculine and feminine in God is now set forth with infinite precision and transferred to the formation of the last two *partsufim* and the relation between them. By and large, *ze'ir* corresponds to the God of revelation in traditional Judaism. He is the masculine principle, which through the breaking of the vessels has departed from its original unity with the feminine and must now be restored on a new plane and under new aspects. The Lurianic gnosis is concerned chiefly with the interrelation of all those figures, their influence and reflection in everything that takes place below, in the worlds of Creation, Formation, and "Making," which come into being below the sphere of the *Shekhinah*, the last stage of the "world of emanation." Everything that happens in the world of the *partsufim* is repeated with increasing intensity in all the lower worlds. These worlds form in an unbroken flow from the lights which grow steadily dimmer—Luria seems to have held that the tenth *sefirah* of every world, that is, the *Shekhinah*, functions at once as a mirror and filter, which throws back the substance of the lights pouring into it and lets through, or transmits, only their residue and reflection. But, in the present state of things, the world of Making is mixed with the world of demonic powers, or "shells," *kelippoth*, which accounts for the crudely material character of its physical manifestation. In essence—and here we have a pure Neoplatonic conception—the world of nature is purely spiritual. Only the breaking of the vessels, in which everything fell from its proper place, caused it to mingle with the demonic world. Thus to separate them once more is one of the central aims of all striving for the *tikkun*.

The crucial stages of this mission have been entrusted to man. For, though much of the process of restitution has already been carried out in God Himself by the setting up of the *partsufim*, it remains to be completed, according to the plan of Creation, by the last reflection of *Adam Kadmon*, who makes his appearance in the lowest form of "Making" (*'asiyah*) as Adam, the first man of Genesis. For Adam was by nature a purely spiritual figure, a 'great soul,' whose very body was a spiritual substance, an ethereal body, or body of light. The upper potencies still flow into him, though refracted and dimmed in their descent. Thus he was a microcosm reflecting the life of all the worlds. And it was up to him, through the concentrated power of his meditation and spiritual action, to remove from himself all the "fallen sparks" that were still in exile, and to put them in their proper place. If Adam had fulfilled this mission, the cosmic process would have been completed on the first Sabbath, and the *Shekhinah* would have been redeemed from exile, from her separation from the masculine, from *ze'ir*. But Adam failed. His failure is described with the help of various symbols, such as the premature consummation of the union between masculine and feminine, or, in the symbolism of the early Kabbalists, the trampling of the young plants in Paradise and the tearing of the fruit from the tree.

Adam's fall corresponds on the anthropological plane to the breaking of the vessels on the theosophical plane. Everything is thrown into worse confusion than before and it is only then that the mixture of the paradisiacal world of nature with the material world of evil takes on its full significance. Complete redemption was within Adam's grasp—all the more drastic is his fall into the depths of material, demonized nature. Thus in the symbolism of Adam's banishment from Paradise, human history begins with exile. Again the sparks of the *Shekhinah* are everywhere, scattered among all the spheres of metaphysical and physical existence. But that is not all. Adam's 'great soul,' in which the entire soul substance of mankind was concentrated, has also shattered. The first man, with his vast cosmic structure, shrinks to his present dimensions. The sparks of Adam's soul and the sparks of the *Shekhinah* disperse, fall, and go into exile where they will be dominated by the "shells," the *kelippoth*. The world of nature and of human existence is the scene of the soul's exile. Each sin repeats the primordial event in part, just as each good deed contributes to the homecoming of the banished souls. Luria draws on Biblical history as an illustration of this process. Everything that happens reflects observance or nonobservance of the secret law of the *tikkun*. At every stage Biblical history offers an opportunity for redemption, but at the decisive point man always fails to take advantage of it. At the highest point in his striving, the exodus of Israel from Egypt and the Revelation on Mount Sinai, man is brought down again by his worship of the golden calf. But the essential function of the Law, both of the Noahide law binding on all men and of the Torah imposed specially upon Israel, is to serve as an instrument of the *tikkun*. Every man who acts in accordance with this Law brings home the fallen sparks of the *Shekhinah* and of his own soul as well. He restores the pristine perfection of his own spiritual body. Seen from this vantage point, the existence and destiny of Israel, with all their terrible reality, with all their intricate drama of ever renewed calling and ever renewed guilt, are fundamentally a symbol of the true state of all being, including—though this was seldom said without reservations—divine being. Precisely because the real existence of Israel is so completely an experience of exile, it is at the same time symbolic and transparent. Thus in its mythical aspect the exile of Israel ceases to be only a punishment for error or a test of faith. It becomes something greater and deeper, a symbolic mission. In the course of its exile Israel must go everywhere, to every corner of the world, for everywhere a spark of the *Shekhinah* is waiting to be found, gathered, and restored by a religious act. And so, surprisingly enough, still meaningfully anchored in the center of a profoundly Jewish gnosis, the idea of exile as a mission makes its appearance. Disintegrating Kabbalism was to bequeath this idea to the rationalistic Judaism of the nineteenth and twentieth centuries. It had lost its deeper meaning, but even then it preserved a vestige of its enormous resonance.

But the exile of the body in outward history has its parallel in the exile of the soul in its migrations from embodiment to embodiment, from one form of being to another. The doctrine of metempsychosis as the exile of the soul acquired unprecedented popularity among the Jewish masses of the generations following the Lurianic period.

In submitting to the guidance of the Law, Israel works toward the restitution of all things. But to bring about the *tikkun* and the corresponding state of the cosmos is precisely the aim of redemption. In redemption everything is restored to its place by the secret magic of human acts, things are freed from their mixture and consequently, in the realms both of man and of nature, from their servitude to the demonic powers, which, once the light is removed from them, are reduced to deathly passivity. In a sense the *tikkun* is not so much a restoration of Creation—which though planned was never fully carried out—as its first complete fulfillment.

Thus fundamentally every man and especially every Jew participates in the process of the *tikkun*. This enables us to understand why in Kabbalistic myth the Messiah becomes a mere symbol, a pledge of the Messianic redemption of all things from their exile. For it is not the act of the Messiah as executor of the *tikkun*, as a person entrusted with the specific function of redemption, that brings Redemption, but your action and mine. Thus for all its setbacks the history of mankind in its exile is looked upon as a steady progress toward the Messianic end. Redemption is no longer looked upon as a catastrophe, in which history itself comes to an end, but as the logical consequence of a process in which we are all participants. To Luria the coming of the Messiah means no more than a signature under a document that we ourselves write; he merely confirms the inception of a condition that he himself has not brought about.

Thus the Lurianic Kabbalah is a great "myth of exile and redemption." And it is precisely this bond with the experience of the Jewish people that gave it its enormous power and its enormous influence on the following generations of Jews.

We have come to the end of this brief exposition. We have seen how the Jews built their historical experience into their cosmogony. Kabbalistic myth had "meaning," because it sprang from a fully conscious relation to a reality which, experienced symbolically even in its horror, was able to project mighty symbols of Jewish life as an extreme case of human life pure and simple. We can no longer fully perceive, I might say, "live," the symbols of the Kabbalah without a considerable effort, if at all. We confront the old questions in a new way. But if symbols spring from a reality that is pregnant with feeling and illumined by the colorless light of intuition, and if, as has been said, all *fulfilled* time is mythical, then surely we may say this: what greater opportunity has the Jewish people ever had than in the horror of defeat, in the struggle and victory of these last years, in its utopian withdrawal into its own history, to fulfil its encounter with its own genius, its true and "perfect nature"?

Introductory Note to a Lurianic Prayerbook

With the text which follows, Jewish mystical praxis reached its most complex and most obscure forms. Before we consider why this was so, we must familiarize ourselves with this type of literature.

Briefly, the theology behind this type of prayer is as follows: In the beginning, there was only God. And God decided to create the cosmos. So He withdrew some of Himself into Himself (*tsimtsum*), creating thereby a realm of transcendental space-time (*tehiru*). This realm, because it was finite, had inherent in it the principle of finitute, of limitedness. Then God caused His light to penetrate into this realm. But His light was infinite and could not be contained by the finitude of the realm of transcendental space-time. So the light and the forms of finitude which had tried to contain it shattered (*shevirah*), leaving fragments of finitude (*kelippot*) and fragments of divine light ("sparks"). God, however, tried again and caused His light to penetrate the realm of transcendental space-time once more (God's *tikkun* of Himself). This time He succeeded in balancing the infinity of His being against the finitude of His cosmos, and He formed ten sefirot. These ten sefirot are the "World of Emanation." These ten sefirot interacted with one another and overflowed into another set of ten sefirot, lower in rank and purity than themselves. The second set of ten sefirot bear the same names as the first set, but they comprise the "World of Creation." The second set generated a third set, called the "World of Formation." And the third set generated a fourth set, called the "World of Making." The fourth set generated the world of the angels and the physical world in which man exists. In this last world, Adam was set. Before his fall, Adam was a very spiritual being, and his task was to gather the sparks which had been scattered through the worlds and to return the sparks to the Godhead (Adam's *tikkun*). Adam, however, failed, and mankind was condemned to its current existence. It is still the task of man, however, to redeem the sparks wherever he can find them, and to return them (through meditation) to the Godhead (man's *tikkun*). If man succeeds, he will redeem himself, the Jewish people, the cosmos, and even God Himself. True prayer is, thus, an act of directed consciousness (*kavvana*) which seeks to raise the sparks through the sefirot of the various worlds (i.e., through the configurations of the sefirot of the various worlds).

The text given here is taken from the prayerbook of Rabbi Shalom Shar'abi (d. 1777), and I have chosen it because it embodies clearly the very complex Lurianic meditative system. Actually, it is a small section from the meditation recited before (and during) *Barukh She-'amar*. *Barukh She-'amar* is the prayer in the daily morning liturgy which introduces the Psalms of praise. The prayer itself is pre-Lurianic, and in the Lurianic version it contains the word *Barukh* ("blessed") thirteen times. Numerologically, thirteen is the number of the attributes of God, and it is also the numerical value of the word *'ehad* ("one"). The purpose of the meditation is to release the sparks in the word *Barukh*.

The text has two parts. The first part is a sefirotic meditation, and the symbolism is to be deciphered as follows: Da'at is one of the ten sefirot in some systems. It comes after Bina. Father and Mother refer to Hokhma and Bina. 'Arikh 'Anpin appears to refer to Hokhma, and its "female counterpart" is Bina. Ze'ir 'Anpin appears to refer to Tiferet, and its female counterpart is Malkhut. The Kings are the sefirot taken together, and the Holy of Holies is the sefirotic realm. Concerning the four worlds: they are, in descending order—'Aṣilut, Beri'a, Yeṣira, and 'Asiya. Note the image-within-image-within-image effect. It is as if four chandeliers composed of pieces of mirror stood in a fully mirrored hallway.

The second part of this passage is of a different character. It is a body meditation, using sounds, Names, and numerology. As to the vowel sounds: The basic vowel-sounds are: *a* (as in *father*), *ei/ey* (as in *hay*), *o* (as in *old*), *e* (as in *fed*), *i* (as in *feed*), and *oo* (as in *food*). According to traditional medieval grammar, most of these vowel-sounds can be long vowels (signified by a straight line over the vowel) or short vowels (signified by a curved line over the vowel). The reader must also know that Hebrew is composed of consonants as well as vowel-sounds. The latter are sometimes written as dots and dashes around the letters, and sometimes certain consonants can denote a vowel. Normally any consonant can be combined with any vowel-sound. In the text, the capital letters represent consonants (including those consonants which represent vowels) while the vowel-sounds are written with lower-case letters. Thus, VaV means that there are two consonants with the sound *v* and between them a vowel with the sound *a*, and YOD means that there are three consonants, the middle of which also represents a vowel. The apostrophe is the usual designation for the letter Aleph, which is the sound we make between the letters *o* in the word *cooperation*. (Actually, it is a brief constriction of the throat—a glottal stop in technical language.) The last thing the reader must know about the alphabet is that each of the letters has a name, for just as the letter *a* in

English is called "Aee," so the first letter in Hebrew is called Aleph. And so on through the alphabet. The consonants of the Tegragrammaton (YHVH), then, are called: Yod, Hey, Vav, Hey, while the consonants of the name 'DNY are called: Aleph, Daled, Nun, Yod.

It is interesting to note that the actual pronunciation of the Tetragrammaton (YHVH) was repressed by the rabbis rather early in the history of Rabbinic Judaism because the people were, apparently, using the Name for magical purposes. So we no longer know how that Name was pronounced. Modern scholars have reconstructed the pronunciation and think it to be *YaHVeH* (meaning "He Who causes to be"). Rabbinic tradition, however, took one of the other Names of God, *'aDoNaY,* which means "my Lord" (and could be used of people too), and substituted it for the now unpronounceable Tetragrammaton. Thus, whenever the Tetragrammaton is written, *'aDoNaY* is read, even to this day. Interestingly enough, certain Christian groups chose to use the consonants of the Tetragrammaton with the vowel-sounds of *'aDoNaY* and formed the hybrid word *YaHoVaH,* also spelled *Jehovah.*

As to the Names: The basic Name is the Tetragrammaton (YHVH), the consonants of which are pronounced with different vowel-sound sequences in the text. The passage also contains the Names 'El, 'ADONAY, and 'EHEYEH. The letters of these Names and their numerical equivalents are interwoven with one another, the best-known combination being Y'HDVNHY, which is YHVH and 'DNY spelled with alternating letters. Since YHVH represents Tiferet and 'DNY represents Malkhut, the combined spelling represents the union of these two sefirot. This combination can also represent, as the text indicates, the union of sound and meaning which we call "speech."

As to the numerology: The reader must know that every letter in the Hebrew alphabet has a numerical value as follows:

'	1	H	5	Ṭ	9	M	40	P	80	SH	300
B	2	V	6	Y	10	N	50	Ṣ	90	T	400
G	3	Z	7	K	20	S	60	Q	100		
D	4	Ḥ	8	L	30	'	70	R	200		

This means that every word has a numerical value. Thus YHVH is equal to 10 plus 5 plus 6 plus 5, which equals 26. By the simple rule that words equal to the same value are "equal" to each other (i.e., substitution is possible), a whole field of numerological-alphabetological inquiry is opened. This field is called *gematria* (a poor man's comprehension of what geometry was). It also means that, since each letter has a name which can be spelled, the spelled-out name of the letter also has a numerological equivalent. Thus, the letter *y* is called YOD and has a numerical value of 10 plus 6 plus 4, which equals 20. Furthermore, as the passage indicates, numerological equivalences can be added, subtracted, etc. Only the capital letters (i.e., the consonants and consonants representing vowel-sounds) can be computed. Just for the record, are the *gematriot* listed in the passage accurate?

In approaching this selection, the reader will want to study it carefully. Not all of it will be clear, but with work, most of it will yield to human understanding. Note the fusion of numerological, body, and theosophic techniques and themes. Note, too, that if you look at the reproduction from this prayerbook (Fig. 12), you will see that it is arranged on the page in the form of a face. There are also questions the reader will want to pose: Why is this material so involuted, so complex? What is the mystic trying to achieve? To what would this praxis lead if it were given free rein to follow its own inner logic? Does it correspond to our conception, or awareness, of the divine? Why; why not? Can a "modern" person be this kind of mystic? Why; why not?

A LURIANIC MEDITATION

סידור תפלה להרש"ש

יכוין לעשות עצמו מרכבה וכסא לאדם דילידה דקדושה.

גלגלתא

מוח שמאל בינה		כתר		מוח ימין חכמה
יְהֹוָה		יְהֹוָה		יְהֹוָה
		דעת עליון		
אֵן שׂמאל		יוד הי ואו הי יוד הי ואו הי		אֵן ימין
יוד הי ואו הה		יוד הי ואו הי יוד הי ואו הי		יוד הי ואוהה
כמס' אֵל יְהֹוָה ע"ה		יוד הי ואו הי יוד הי ואו הי		כמס' אֵל יְהֹוָה ע"ה
עין שמאל ילידה		דעת תחתון יְהֹוָה יְהֹוָה		עין ימין ילידה

	חוטם	
יוד הא ואו הא	נקב ימין נקב שמאל	יוד הא ואו הא
יוד הא ואו הא		יוד הא ואו הא
יוד הא ואו הא		יוד הא ואו הא
יוד הא ואו הא		יוד הא ואו הא
יוד הא ואו הא		יוד הא ואו חא

אֱהֹיֶה אֱהֹיֶה אֱהֹיֶה חילו'

אֱהֹדֹיְהֹוָה אֱהֹיֶה חוטם פס ד' אותיות והכו' גי' מייט.

פֶּה

גי' ס"ג וכ"ב אותיות דס' מולאות הפס יוד הי ואו הי
אחהי"ע גיכ"ק דטלנ"ת זסשרי"ץ זסשרי"ץ בומ"ף

יוד הי ואו הי אהיה פנימיות הפה
יוד יוד הא יוד הא ואו גי' פ"ס מילוגיות

קוֹל יְהֹוָה, גי' יופיא"ל ע"ה דְּבּוּר אֲדֹנָי
קוֹל וַדִבּוּר יֹאהֹדֹוָנַהֹי

דִּבּוּר גי' כ"ו מ"ה ק"ל ועשר אותיות והכולל.
יהוה יוד הא ואו הא מספר ואותיות. ס"ה פ"א
יוד יוד הא יוד הא ואו יוד הא ואו הא ק"ל

זרוע שמאל גבורה		נופח ח"ח		זרוע ימין חסד
יְהֹוָה		יְהֹוָה		יְהֹוָה
שוק שמאל הוד		ברית יסד		שוק ימין נצח
יְהֹוָה		יֹהֹוֹוֹהֹוּ		יְהֹוָה
רגל שמאל גי'		עטרת היסוד		רגל ימין גי'
	טל יְהֹוָה		

יוד אלף הי הי ויו יוד הי הי :   יוד אלף הי הי ויו יוד הי הי

A page from *Siddur Rashash.*

Fig. 12

A Meditation Before Barukh She-'amar

From the *Siddur Rashash*

One should intend to conjoin Keter, Hokhma, Binah, and Da'at of [the worlds of] 'Asiyah, Yesira, and Beri'a with 'Arikh 'Anpin and its female counterpart; [with] the Father and the Mother; and [with] Ze'ir 'Anpin and its female counterpart [each of which is of the world] of Yesira [as reflected in the world of] 'Asilut. They [i.e., the latter set] are contained in the configurations opposite them in Yesira. [And one should intend] to draw from them the soul-spirit-pneuma-anima-psyche of the inner spirit and mind [which] encompasses the mediate vessels of Ze'ir 'Anpin and its female counterpart of each of them [i.e., of the worlds] in order to purge the mediate vessels such as Hokhma-Binah-Da'at of the Kings of each of them [i.e., each of the worlds]; [and in order] to raise them together with the purged vessels [which are] the external aspect of Nesah-Hod-Yesod of the Kings together with the internal aspect of Yesira and 'Asiya with its soul-spirit; and [in order] to encompass and raise together with them the external aspect Yesira and 'Asiya [which are] internal to, and encompass, Beri'a. [All this] by means of the palaces of Ze'ir 'Anpin of Yesira, as mentioned above, for each one of them—raising it from palace to palace until Beri'a. This [is done] by [recitation of] the Psalms.

One should say *Barukh She-'amar,* in which the word *Barukh* is [mentioned] thirteen times corresponding to [the value of the word] *'ehad,* in order to unify the head of 'Arikh 'Anpin which is the palace of Holy of Holies of 'Arikh 'Anpin of Yesira with the head of 'Asiya. Included in it [i.e., in the prayer *Barukh She-'amar*] are eighty-seven words corresponding to the thirteen restorations of the beard of 'Anikh 'Anpin plus the nine [restorations] of Ze'ir 'Anpin, plus the [value of the] Name *'adonay* of its [*Ze'ir 'Anpin's*] corresponding female [i.e., $13 + 9 + (1 + 4 + 50 + 10) = 87$]. This Ze'ir 'Anpin and its corresponding female constitute the roots of Ze'ir 'Anpin and its corresponding female, which are dependent upon 'Arikh 'Anpin. The intent one should have in [reciting] the thirteen [words] *Barukh* is to [draw] light from the thirteen restorations of the beard of 'Arikh 'Anpin

174

to the nine [restorations] of Ze'ir 'Anpin and [from there] to the Name 'aDoNaY of its corresponding female. And all of this with the external aspect which is the beard. However, concerning the internal aspect, one should intend these eighty-seven letters for the sake of Mah [Hokhma] and for the forty-two letters of the simple and full, and the completely full [spelling of the Name] of Mah.

One should also intend to make oneself into a Chariot and a Throne for the Adam of the Yesira of holiness as follows: The skull is Keter [and one meditates/recites]—YaHaVaHa. [On a lower level, the skull is also] Supernal Knowledge [and one meditates] Yod Hey Vav Hey [seven times]. [On a lower level still, the skull] is Lower Knowledge [and one meditates] YoHeiVaHei [twice].

The right [side] of the brain is Hokhma [and one meditates] YaHaVaHa. [It is also the] right ear [and one meditates] YOD HeY VAV HAH, which is the numerical [equivalent] of 'eL-YHVH plus one for the word [itself, i.e., 57 + 1]. [It is also] the right eye of Yesira [and one meditates] YoD Hei' VaV Hei' [five times].

The left [side] of the brain is Binah [and one meditates] Yei Hei Vei Hei. [It is also] the left ear [and one meditates] YOD HeY VAV HaH, which is the numerical [equivalent] of 'el-YHVH plus one for the word [itself]. [It is also] the left eye of Yesira [and one meditates] YoD Hei' VAV Hei' [five times].

The nose: [For] the internal aspect of the right nostril [one meditates] YoD HeY VaV HeY. [For] the internal aspect of the left nostril [one meditates] YoD HeY VaV HeY. [For] the external aspect [of the nose one meditates] 'HYH [three times and] 'HYH YHVH 'HYH. The numerical value of [the word for nose] HOTeM plus four for the four letters [of the word] plus one for the intent equals [the value of the word "life"] ḤaYYiM.

The mouth: The numerical equivalent of [the word for mouth] PeH is [85]: sixty-three [which is the sum of] YOD HeY VAV HeY, which are the five basic sounds of the mouth, plus twenty-two [which is the number of] letters [of the alphabet]: 'ḤH' GYKQ DṬLNT ZSShRṢ BVMP. [The meditation for] the internal aspect of the mouth [is] YoD HeY VaV HeY 'HYH. [For] the external aspect [it is] YOD YOD Hei' YOD Hei' VAV which has the numerical equivalent of PeH [mouth, i.e., 85].

Voice, the numerical equivalent of QOL ["sound"] being the same as that of YOFY'eL [an angel] plus one for the word [itself, i.e., 135 + 1], is YHVH. Speech is 'DNY. [Thus], sound and speech [together] are Y'HDVNHY [i.e., the two names of God spelled together with alternating letters]. Speech [DiBUR, which is 212] has a numerical equivalent [as follows]: YHVH [which is] 26, plus YOD Hei' VAV Hei' [which is] 45, plus 10 for the ten letters [of that expansion], plus YOD YOD Hei' YOD Hei' VAV YOD Hei' VAV Hei' [which is] 130, plus one for the sum.

The right arm is Hesed [and one meditates] YeHeVeHe. The right thigh is Nesah [and one meditates] YiHiViHi. The [meditation for the] right foot is YOD 'aLeF HeY HeY Va'V YOD HeY HeY [which is] the numerical equivalent of ReGeL ["foot" i.e., 233].

The left arm is Gevurah [and one meditates] YiHiViHi. The left thigh is Hod [and one meditates] Yoo Hoo Voo Hoo. The [meditation for the] left foot is YOD 'aLeF HeY HeY Va'V YOD HeY HeY [which is the numerical equivalent of ReGeL ["foot," i.e., 233].

The torso is Tiferet [and one meditates] YoHoVoHo. [On a lower level,] the covenantal organ is Yesod [and one meditates] Yoo Hoo Voo Hoo. [On a lower level], the crown of Yesod is Malkhut [and one meditates] YiHaVoH.

Conclusion

Lurianic Kabbala, both in its ideas and in its praxis, was a very powerful and influential force for several centuries. Christian Kabbala, Jewish mystical messianism, Reform Judaism, secular Jewish nationalism, and Hasidism all owe debts to Lurianic Kabbala. What was the secret of its power? Why was it so influential? And what happened to it, for it is not a central element in modern Judaism?

The importance of Lurianic Kabbala lies in two major insights. First, the repersonalization of God begun in the Zohar is, in the Lurianic development, carried further. The reader will recall that in the Zohar, God was conceived as a being possessed of personality, of consciousness; and that in conceiving God this way, the Zohar was in effect returning to the personalist view of God of the Bible and early Rabbinic Judaism. The new perspective of the Zohar on this matter was that God not only shared consciousness with mankind. He also shared some of humankind's impotence. God and man were conceived as being mutually dependent. Each was seen as helping the other to achieve ontological fulfillment and as capable of impeding the other's fulfillment. Luria took this idea one step further and taught that God, even before the creation of man, is a being Who must wrestle with His own transcendence in order to put it into containable form. God cannot simply will His manifestations into being. Nor can He simply allow them to flow smoothly from Him. Rather, He must wrestle, strive, and fight to balance reality against the forces of the spirit. Furthermore, Luria taught, this striving is a violent process. It is a shattering of conceptions, a fragmentizing of the self. This sense of inner, violent struggle in God and the subsequent fragmentizing of the divine is one of the most powerful ideas in theological thinking in any age. No wonder it captured the imagination of so many! In conceiving God in this fashion, however, Luria simply extended the anthropopathic understanding of God one step beyond the Zohar, and one step closer to our own perception of the dynamics of human consciousness. For creative living is, indeed, a wrestling of the spiritual into form. Creation of any kind is,

177

indeed, a fragmentizing of the original unity into discrete, manageable parts. Self-articulation *is* a violent, self-fragmenting process. Furthermore, although the articulated self is graspable, it is "in exile." It is separated from the primordial unity of consciousness. And therefore, Luria taught, even after striving successfully to articulate the self, God (and man) yearns for the return of the primal unity. God, and man, seek redemption from self-fragmentation, from self-exile. Lurianic Kabbala is, thus, truly a theology (and psychology) of violent self-fragmentation and intense yearning for inner restoration.

The second major insight of Lurianic Kabbala is the messianic radicalization of man. The reader will recall that, in the Zohar, the responsibility for the ongoing welfare of God fell to mankind. Luria took this idea further (as the reading from Scholem makes clear) and taught that the restoration of the primordial wholeness to God, to the cosmos, and to man lie in the hands of man. Luria taught that it is the individual mystic who is the Messiah because it is he who returns the "sparks" to the divine. It is he who restores unity to God and the world. This idea is truly anarchic in its potential, and Scholem has traced this line of development in several of his works.

Why, then, did Lurianic Kabbala not survive? Actually, it did survive. I have myself been present in a synagogue in Jerusalem where Lurianic prayerbooks were in use. Furthermore, it is likely that Lurianic praxis is carried on in Hasidic circles, but only by the leaders (the Zaddikim). However, it is generally true that Lurianic Kabbala faded into the background, even of Jewish mystical tradition. The reasons for this are not hard to understand: Lurianic theory is exceptionally complex. For instance, each "world" contains ten sefirot, and each sefira reflects all the other sefirot in all the other worlds. This yields a total of 40^4, or 2,560,000 combinations. To meditate one's way up that ladder is quite a task. Similarly, Lurianic praxis became exceptionally complex. The meditations of the *Siddur Rashash,* only a small page of which was translated above, are incredibly convoluted and the *kavvanot* for various occasions are endless. It is also true that the association of Lurianic praxis with the freeing of reincarnated souls and other acts which to the Western mind are sheer superstition added to the desuetude into which Lurianic Kabbala fell.

What, then, did happen to Lurianic Kabbala? How did it develop and influence later ideas and movements? The influence of Lurianic Kabbala can be seen in four areas: in Christian Kabbala, in Sabbatianism, in modern Reform and secular-nationalist Judaism, and in Hasidism. It is beyond the scope of this book to deal with Christian Kabbala. The interested reader can begin with the encyclopedia articles and proceed to the learned books on the subject.

The term "Sabbatianism" refers to the ideas and the movement generated by the mystical false-Messiah, Sabbatai Zevi. Briefly, Sabbatai

Zevi was proclaimed the Messiah in 1666 C.E., and in 1667, confronted with the threat of execution, he converted to Islam. Many of his followers (and he had a massive following among the Jews of his time) left him, but many remained loyal, still considering him to be the true Messiah. What enabled these followers to view a man who had become an apostate as the true Messiah? Basically, it was a Lurianic idea. Luria had taught the need to "redeem the sparks," and the followers of Sabbatai Zevi extended this as follows: To fully accomplish his task, the Messiah must descend into the realm of error and impurity in order to "redeem the sparks" that are there. In becoming an apostate, then, Sabbatai Zevi was seen only to be following the logic of the Lurianic definition of redemption. Interestingly enough, a century after Sabbatai Zevi, a figure appeared in Europe who utilized much the same line of reasoning to urge conversion to Christianity. Another Sabbatian extension of Lurianic thought is in the realm of sin. Luria had taught that "sparks" are contained also in sins. Sabbatai Zevi and his followers argued that only by actually committing these sins could one "redeem the sparks" hidden therein. This reasoning led to ritual consumption of forbidden foods and, in later Sabbatianism, even to ritual adultery. Here, too, the theory and praxis of Sabbatianism were only a logical extension of the Lurianic definition of redemption. All this, strange as it may seem, has been well documented by G. Scholem in his various works. The interested reader should consult them, especially *The Messianic Idea in Judaism*.

Scholem has courageously followed the implications of Sabbatianism and its historical traces up into the modern period. He has shown the juxtaposition of repressed Sabbatianism with the French Revolution. He has also argued that the Sabbatian logic had completely undermined the usual rabbinic assumptions about authoritative Judaism by the onset of the modern period, and that the radical theology and practice which characterize modern Judaism grow out of the radical theology and praxis of Sabbatianism. A certain readiness for change, Scholem has argued, was inherent in Judaism as it entered the modern period *because of* Sabbatian thought and praxis, which had been anti-rabbinic, and which had reversed many of the traditional rabbinic values. In a word, the anarchism preached and practiced by the followers of Sabbatianism with respect to rabbinic tradition and authority prepared the way for the anti-rabbinic, anti-traditional forms of modern Judaism, both the Re-forms as well as the secularized forms. For a fuller statement of the argument and the presentation of the evidence, the interested reader should consult Scholem's works, especially *The Messianic Idea*.

The fourth area in which Lurianic influence can be felt is in modern Hasidism. Here, the net effect appears to be one of simplification in theory and in praxis. First, Hasidism developed the idea of the Eyn Sof. The reader will recall that, in Zoharic and Lurianic Kabbala, the Eyn Sof is the unknowable, infinite, remotest aspect of God. In Hasidism it is still that, but it is also seen as an all-embracing being (in some traditions) or as the being on the other side of the great Nothing (in other traditions). Second, Hasidism developed a "split-level" spirituality, with the Zaddik (the leader) being the one who practices Lurianic *kavvanot* (and, even then, not as a central mode of worship), while the Hasid (the follower) practices a more direct, less convoluted type of spirituality. And third, Hasidism preserved the idea of the "sparks" being everywhere. The need to sin and to become an apostate was, of course, rejected. But the readiness to see God in any and every moment of human experience is a characteristic attitude of Hasidism, the roots of which are in the Lurianic tradition.

11

GENERAL CONCLUSION

Our study of the Zoharic stream of Jewish mysticism has revealed to us a world at least as strange as that of Merkabah mysticism. In many ways, its authors speak to us even more profoundly than the authors of the Merkabah tradition. Why is this so? What is the enchantment of the Zoharic tradition?

The enchantment of the Zoharic tradition lies foremost in the conception of God that is portrayed in the literature. We have seen that this tradition purports to speak of the intimate consciousness of God, of the inner workings of His personality. And as beings possessed of consciousness and personality, we are curious, and I would even say have a need, to try to grasp God in the terms which are most familiar, and most distinctive, to us. We know that our personal consciousness is what gives us our intimate identity, and so we feel that if we could know God that way, then we would have a more intimate knowledge of Him. We feel that by probing God's personality, we will have a truer knowledge of what He and we are really like. God is there, somewhere, undefined, in the background of our being. Zoharic tradition enables us to speak of Him in powerful and intimate terms. It enables us to grapple with God face to face, heart to heart, and mind to mind. And, therefore, it is a powerful analytic tool, a meaningful religious Way. It is the same realization of the centrality of human consciousness that motivates sensitive persons to try to grapple with the human situation through the use of psychoanalysis, for psychoanalysis, too, purports to speak of the human personality and its intimate levels of consciousness. (D. Bakan, in his *Sigmund Freud and the Jewish Mystical Tradition,* even went so far as to indicate that Freud may have drawn some of his ideas from the Zoharic stream of Jewish mysticism.)

Furthermore, we have seen that the Zoharic tradition teaches that God's consciousness is characterized by an unstable mixture of conflicting impulses. This idea, too, is very powerful (and there are a host of other

181

ideas that we have not been able to explore which are equally as powerful) because it shows us clearly that God is not the superman-in-the-sky. He is not the great-heavenly-magician. Rather, God is a being, and insofar as He interacts with the finite world, He too is limited. Furthermore, God is a conscious being. True, He is more powerful, more knowing, but He too, as a being possessed of articulate consciousness, must contend with conflicting ideas within Himself, with conflicting desiderata, with conflicting paths of action. He is not above all conflict. He is not the tranquil-sea-in-the-sky, the motionless-puddle-in-eternity. He is not the beauteous-being-in-beatific-repose. He is the Creator, the Judge. He *must* confront facts and reach decisions, some of them very difficult. How can he *not* be in conflict?

Another reason for the enchantment of the Zoharic tradition lies in its teachings about the relationship between God and man, for the Zoharic tradition teaches that the stability of the mixture of God's conflicting impulses is influenced by the behavior of man, for better and for worse. Here again we have a very powerful idea because we are being taught that God is not the imperturbable Father Who metes out justice (or love) when life is all over. He is not the withdrawn Almighty Who hovers in the background until His turn comes to even the score by either an act of grace or an act of just retribution. Rather, He is the involved Father Whose breath of life is choked off by evil and Whose joy streams forth in response to good. He is the engagé Parent Who aggravates Himself into impotence when His children act stupidly and Who experiences inner joy when they evidence genuine insight in what they do and say. The Zohar further teaches that God is not only a real-life Father but also a Mother (Malkhut). Here, too, God is not a Cinderella-type stepmother, nor a fountain perpetually flowing with milk and honey. Rather, God is a real-life Mother—sometimes good to us, sometimes bad; sometimes just, sometimes irrational; but always engaged, always concerned, always subject to the feelings and acts that are directed toward Him/Her. No wonder the Zoharic tradition is so enchanting! It may deprive us of our omnipotent-, impersonal-force conception of God, but it gives us a much more human, conscious, concerned being to deal with.

There are other reasons for the enchanting quality of the Zoharic tradition. It *is* a highly imaginative way of thinking, and in a world in which religion is often reduced to an act of mind or of cult, or to a social or political act, a religious perspective with some imagination is much to be appreciated. The Zoharic tradition is also a deeply symbolic system, and in a world devoted to journalism, symbolic thinking and communication are also to be appreciated. The Zoharic tradition is also a deeply mythic tradition. By this I mean that, even in its symbols, and perhaps because of them, Zoharic literature speaks to very deep levels of human need. With a quick turn of phrase, we find ourselves deep in the midst of worlds quite remote from everyday reality and yet quite relevant to our deepest understanding of ourselves and of God. This symbolic-mythic-poetic dimension of the Zoharic tradition is partly responsible for its enchanting quality.

Why, then, is the Zoharic tradition not more popular? Here too there are several reasons. First, the tradition is largely unknown, for although parts of the tradition are available in English, the skills of interpretation are largely unknown. Second, our society is, in large measure, an anti-intellectual, anti-spiritual society, and so, even if the literature and the skills were known, they would not be popular. More important than these "objective" reasons, however, is the realization that somewhere inside us, we would rather have a conception of God as an omnipotent-impersonal-force. If God is remote, He can make no demands. If God is out-there-somewhere, we need not deal with Him now and maybe not even later. If God's power is absolute, then we can "have faith" in Him to straighten things out in the end. But if God is not remote, then it is we who must take responsibility for the relationship. If God is not omnipotent, then it is we who must care for our Parent. If God's power is limited, it is we who must share the burden of governance. Not many of us really want these burdens, and so the Zoharic tradition is not likely to flourish, even if the knowledge and the skills can be communicated.

Interestingly enough, in rabbinic circles it was forbidden to study the Zohar until after one was settled, that is, until after one was over thirty years old, married, and employed. Some say the reason for this is the explicit sexual imagery. I am inclined to doubt it because young men studied other explicit texts in the law codes, and so on. I think it is because of the conception of God contained in this tradition, for a conception of God which purports to explain His intimate consciousness, which speaks of Him as an unstable mixture of conflicting impulses, and which shows Him to be dependent upon man is indeed a conception that cannot be presented to one who is immature. Furthermore, a conception of the God-man relationship which assigns the major share to man is also an idea not meant for immature minds. The secret of the entire Zoharic tradition, then, lies, as the rabbis properly saw, in its radical portrayal of the nature of God and in the radical role it assigned to man. The Zoharic tradition is truly an esoteric tradition, a secret knowledge restricted to the select few.

Because of its esoteric nature and because of the complexification it underwent over the centuries, the Zoharic tradition faded into the background of the Jewish mystical tradition. New world-views were to arise which would be less arcane, less obscure. New conceptions of mysticism were to arise which would be more accessible to the masses.

New practices were to arise which would place much greater emphasis on ecstatic experiences, and it is these practices which would capture the religious imagination of the people, scholars and masses alike. It is to these ecstatic traditions that we ought to turn next.

AFTERWORD

In the Foreword to this book, I set three problems for the reader: (1) to identify the terms and images in these texts which form the universe of spiritual discourse and to try to differentiate the types of spirituality in these texts one from another; (2) to speculate upon the point at which one can legitimately use the word "mystical" in relation to these texts; and (3) to determine that which is specifically "Jewish" about these texts or, more elegantly, to determine in what way these texts were influenced by, and in turn influenced, Rabbinic Judaism, in the midst of which they flourished. We are now prepared to venture some answers to these questions.

In the Merkabah tradition, the terms and images which clearly allude to some spiritual reality are the letters, the hymns, the seals, the crowns, the angels, the magical formulations, the other heavenly creatures, the purity, and so on. I have referred to this type of mysticism as "power mysticism," and the term is apt. The transcendent, or the spiritual, in this tradition is the element of power, the imitation of God through acquisition and use of His creative power. As one of my students so aptly put it: "I can feel the drive of these men to become one with the powers of creation that they sense in the letters and words given by God . . . determinedly and faithfully opening themselves to the power of the words and letters, a divine gift, as a means of unifying their own shadow of God with His creative process."

In the Zoharic tradition, the terms and images which clearly allude to some spiritual reality are the sefirot, the theurgical process, the flow of energy-light, the presence of male and female and the union between them, the very fragmentedness and helplessness of God, and so on. This type of mysticism I have called deeply personalist, not only in the usual sexual and love imagery but in its innermost conception and articulation. The transcendent, or the spiritual, in this tradition is the element of personalism. It is the imitation of God through the concentration of personal energy. It is the entering of a personal, intimate relation with the divine through directed awareness. It is being personally engaged with God on the most intimate levels of our conscious being and of His. As a student

185

remarked, Zoharic mysticism is a seeking of inner balance and union in a universe of self which is essentially in imbalance and disunion. It is a seeking of inner harmony and free flow of inner energy "in order to bless not only myself and the world, but God Himself." All of this is a far cry from the usual types of spirituality present in Rabbinic Judaism.

The second problem I set for the reader was: At what point can we speak of this material as being "mystical"? Interestingly enough, Scholem seems to maintain that there is no conceptual moment at which spirituality shades into mysticism. He has maintained that the criterion must be literary, i.e., that Jewish mysticism can be defined by the literary coherence of the tradition. Nonetheless, I think the question can be fairly posed (as it has been done by F. Heiler for the Christian tradition) as follows: Given the category of spirituality with its forms and dynamics (cf. the Foreword), when do the forms and dynamics of spirituality turn "mystical"? To answer this very difficult scholarly question we must recognize, first, that the views of the mystics to the contrary notwithstanding, mystical dynamics are only a subset of the dynamics of spirituality; that mystical dynamics are not spirituality par excellence but are only part of the larger conceptual range of spirituality. In this, incidentally, I think that rabbinic tradition concurs. Second, we must recognize that both the forms and the dynamics of even mystical spirituality differ considerably from one time and place to another. For instance, the forms and dynamics of Zoharic theurgy differ greatly from the forms and dynamics of ecstatic kabbalism. Given these caveats, I would say that the forms and dynamics of spirituality turn "mystical" when *the reports of the experiences involved betray an abstract conceptualization of God, as opposed to a highly personalist, anthropopathic conceptualization.* I have tried to word this very carefully, writing about "reports" because all we have for analysis is reports. I have written of "experiences" because, while some forms of mystical literature are really types of Talmud and philosophy, it is my firm conviction that most, if not all, of mystical literature reflects actual or anticipated experiences on the part of the writer. Furthermore, and most important, I have written of "experiences," in the plural, for I disagree that mystical experience is one amorphous experience which molds itself into various cultural forms. On the contrary, the literature seems to testify quite unambiguously to different experiences, in the plural, in different contexts; to different types of awareness and consciousness. This differentiation seems to be documented in non-Jewish mysticism as well. I have also written about the reports betraying "conceptualization." By this I do not mean an "idea of God" in any systematic philosophic sense of the word, but a conceptualization—approximate and unsystematic. Furthermore, this conceptualization can be deduced from the materials. It is "betrayed" and not explicitly taught.

Concerning the basic distinction I have made between an "abstract" and a "personalist" conceptualization of God, I would like to point out that Biblical religion, although recognizing the limitations of anthropopathy, conceived spirituality as an experience of the Presence of God—overpowering, awesome, often verbal, sometimes ecstatic—but always it is the Presence of God that forms the core of the experience that is later reduced to words. Similarly, rabbinic religion, as reflected in the liturgy and Halakha about *kavvana,* recognized the limits of anthropopathy, but conceived man's relationship to God as essentially one of presence-to-Presence. God was transcendent, yet through his spiritual capacities, man could sense God, i.e., His personalist Presence. Similarly, the part of the Hasidic tradition represented by Levi Yitzhak's contending with God also betrays a distinctly personalist conceptualization of God. On the other hand, those reports which betray a conceptualization of God as a remote Force which acts through various and sundry intermediaries is nonpersonalist at its core. Thus, the Merkabah literature, highly imagistic as it is, betrays a conceptualization of God as an abstract Force, remote from man, not directly sensible by him. Similarly, the philosophic mysticism of Maimonides betrays a God whose accessibility is limited to the lowest of the Intelligences, even for Moses. Similarly, the God beyond the sefirot of the Zoharic tradition is just that, beyond, abstract (although an attempt to reinterpret the Zoharic sefirot as the "personality" of God and prayer as a form of "therapy" brings that tradition back into the anthropopathic camp). Similarly, the ecstatic traditions of Abulafia and Hasidic *biṭṭul* betray an abstract conceptualization of God.

Is, then, the material we have seen "mystical"? The Merkabah material is certainly that. The Zoharic material, insofar as it presents God as ultimately abstract, is mystical. Also, insofar as it speaks of man's experience of God as abstract and not personal, it is mystical. But insofar as Zoharic tradition conceives God on the model of human consciousness, it is not mystical. Insofar as Zoharic tradition conceives man's relation to God as person-to-person, it is not mystical. It may be "gnostic" in a loose sense of the word, but it is not mystical.

The third problem I set for the reader was to identify the Jewish elements in the Jewish mystical tradition and to speculate on the relationship between mysticism and Rabbinic Judaism. What, then, are the Jewish elements in this literature? First and foremost, we note that this is a very, very learned tradition. The material is very complex. The material presupposes a working knowledge of the Bible and of rabbinic literature. Also, the more the tradition progresses, the more one must know, for the tradition is cumulative. In one way or another, the tradition is really a commentary on the Bible, the Talmud, and the preceding texts in the tradition. Furthermore, these systems of thought are, as we have seen, each deeply rooted in some other thought-system as well, be it Hellenistic magic, Islamic philosophy, some form of mythic thinking, etc. This mysticism was written by and for a highly educated elite. It was written by and for a small group of rabbis. It is also the case that this tradition is learned, in the sense that it is highly verbal. There are no icons, no music, no painting, no poetry. It is rather alphabet- and number-oriented, or personality-oriented. In this learnedness, Jewish mystical tradition contrasts with other traditions, for the illiterate mystic of the East or of Christianity is unknown here. Such a person could not be a Jewish mystic. Furthermore, the emphasis on love mysticism is almost completely missing. Rather, love of God is a function of knowledge, and knowledge is contained in the system. Love is not an overpowering emotion that moves man to tears in God.

A second major characteristic of the Jewish mystical tradition is that it is covenantal, i.e., that it exists within Torah, within Halakha, within Rabbinic Judaism. There is a great deal of tension between mystic and rabbinic authority, for to the mystic it is the experience that validates the communal consensus concerning practice and belief, while for the rabbinic Jew it is the consensus which validates the experience. Yet in spite of this tension, the mystic and the rabbi exist side by side, often in the same person.

Third, Jewish mysticism is hierarchical. The concentric circles of humanity, the Jews, the rabbis, the mystics is one example. The uranography (geography of the heavens) is another. The remoteness of the ultimate stage of God (even the Eyn Sof is ultimately remote and inaccessible) bridged by a series of intermediate stages is another example. In this, the Jewish mystical tradition is Hellenistic and medieval.

Fourth, Jewish mysticism teaches something about God and man. It teaches that God is ultimately remote, yet in the Zoharic tradition, that He needs man in a very intimate way. It teaches that man can be the bearer of his own redemption. But most importantly, Jewish mystical tradition teaches that man, with proper knowledge and proper disciplined praxis, can contact God; that man, with proper knowledge, can tread the Way to God and have contact with Him. In some respects, this is not a new idea, yet if we conceive of prophecy as a seizing of man by God, i.e., if we conceive of the most intense religious experience as being a unilateral act by God, then mysticism represents a new theory of the God-man relationship. For mysticism teaches that man can approach God, i.e., that the process can be reversed, that the highest religious experience is man-initiated.

Lastly, we note that the Jewish mystical tradition is quite diverse. We have seen the power mysticism of magic and visions in the Merkabah tradition and we have seen the personalist mysticism of the Zoharic tradition. The philosophic and ecstatic traditions with their distinctive elements and Hasidism with its "split-level spirituality," which in very many ways turns the major qualities of Jewish mysticism upside down, remain to be explicated.

What of the relationship of the mystic to Rabbinic Judaism?

The relationship of the mystic to society is, at its core, a conflict of religious ideologies. For the Jewish mystic this conflict was, and is, between Rabbinic Judaism on the one hand and mysticism on the other. Briefly, Rabbinic Judaism taught the double-Torah theory, i.e., that both the Written Torah and the Oral Torah were given by God to Moses, and that both were equally valid, with interpretative authority being vested in the rabbis, theologically and practically. Rabbinic Judaism also taught the practice of popular piety—i.e., that the cult, in the broadest sense of the word, was to be practiced by each and every rabbinic Jew, in all places, and at all times. Rabbinic tradition was determined by scholars. It was rational. It guided the community and gave the group coherence and identity. The Passover Haggadah, a classic text of rabbinism, for example, defined the wicked son as one who denies the group and its sacred text. Mysticism, on the other hand, taught that the direct, immediate experience of the divine was the core of religious life, and hence that mystical ecstasy superseded the tradition of revelation. Mystical tradition could be, thus, strongly antinomian and anarchic while rabbinic tradition was strongly nomian and social. These two religious ideologies could only clash with one another, and as the dust settled, syntheses of various proportions were to emerge. Scholem, among others, has done a great deal to set out the battle lines of this clash and to show the development of its dialectic tensions. Unfortunately, however, these analyses have not been set into a general conceptual rubric. I would like to propose, therefore, that the influence exerted by each of these traditions upon the other be classified systematically as the "rabbinization" of mysticism and the "mysticization" of rabbinism. This requires further explanation.

The "rabbinization" of mysticism can be seen briefly in the following three instances: (1) When the clash was irresolvable, the community simply expelled those who did not accept basic "rabbinization," e.g., Elisha ben Abuya, Sabbatai Zevi, and others. The poor reception accorded Martin Buber in rabbinic circles is, in part, due to this. (2) The essentially "non-Jewish" character of the techniques, experiences, metaphors, and symbols of mystical tradition were "rabbinized" when Jewish mystics chose to accept and use the central symbols of Rabbinic Judaism. Thus Torah, liturgy, study, redemption, revelation, creation, law, Israel, etc., all became integral parts of Jewish mysticism. Similarly, the use of exegesis in theosophic mysticism, the reinterpretation of the commandments along mystical lines, etc., are all elements in Jewish mysticism which were superimposed on it by the process of "rabbinization." The very "bookish-ness" of Jewish mysticism is an influence from the rabbinic tradition. (3) The nontheological possibilities of mysticism—as in some Far Eastern mystical traditions—were "rabbinized" when Jewish mystics chose to place their expressions within the universe of theological discourse, within the thoroughly theological world-view of the rabbinic tradition. Thus, the interpretation of the experience of ecstasy as a form of prophecy or prayer, the use of Name-magic in "practical mysticism," the complexities of Zoharic theosophy, the mystical view of salvation, etc., are all set within the conception of a unique and unknowable God. Furthermore, even at its most provocative, the concept of God in the Jewish mystical tradition was seen as having roots in earlier Jewish traditions and as an extension thereof. As a result, Jewish mystical teaching was "rabbinized" in being fully set within that which rabbinic Judaism preached and taught about God.

There are other ways in which mysticism was "rabbinized": the use of verbal and not plastic imagery, the lack of an approved monastic-ascetic tradition, the strong social and cosmic orientation of Zoharic theurgy, etc. More work needs to be done to analyze the data and to set them into a systematic rubric.

What about the other side of the coin? How was Rabbinic Judaism "mysticized?" Here, too, the studies of Scholem are definitive, though not set in an overall framework. Briefly: While in the rabbinic tradition the Torah was a text and its interpretation an exoteric process, under the influence of the mystical tradition the Torah became an aspect of God and its interpretation an esoteric process. While in the rabbinic tradition the object of study was God's revealed will, under the influence of the mystical tradition the object of study came to be God Himself. While in the rabbinic tradition observance was of God's command, under the influence of the mystical tradition observance became a sacrament. While in the rabbinic tradition redemption was a national-political concept, under the influence of the mystical tradition redemption became a personal and cosmic reunification. While in the rabbinic tradition *Kavvana* was a meditation toward the Presence of God, under the influence of the mystical tradition *Kavvana* became a unification of the separated elements of the divine with one another. While in the rabbinic tradition evil was a given of worldly reality deriving mostly from the actions of men, under the influence of the mystical tradition evil became a given of divine reality, originating in the complex workings of the personality of God. While in the rabbinic tradition the experience of ecstasy was latent, in the mystical tradition it came to be much closer to the surface. And so on. In fact, there is hardly a symbol, act, or belief in the rabbinic tradition which was not touched, and transformed, by the mystical tradition.

The evidence offered here is sufficient to demonstrate that the mystical tradition, in spite of its "non-Jewish" and even anti-rabbinic characteristics, was able to coexist with the rabbinic tradition, in spite of the latter's avowedly exoteric and social character. In fact, there is a certain interpenetration which goes so deep that one can properly speak of a "rabbinic mysticism" (or, as the Orthodox literature of today puts it, a "Torah mysticism"). So much so, that the rabbinic-judicial-scholarly elite and the mystical elite are almost always identical. So much so, that even the common rabbinic Jew aspires to be a "rabbinic mystic." So much so, that every rabbinic Jew is taught to recognize that the distinctively religious impulse of his commitment must derive from his "Jewish mysticism."

The texts have been presented and explicated. The words and images of spirituality have been illustrated. The types of spirituality have been set forth. A definition of the mystical as a distinct subset of the spiritual has been proposed. The Jewish elements have been identified. And an interpretation of the relationship between Rabbinic Judaism and mysticism has been set forth. It remains only for the reader to follow the rabbinic injunction, "Go forth and learn."

FOR FURTHER READING

There is no reading that can be done in the field of Jewish mysticism without studying the works of G. Scholem. First and foremost, for a history of Jewish mysticism, one must read his *Major Trends in Jewish Mysticism*. Second, for studies in mystical symbolism, in the relationship of the mystical and the normative traditions, and so on, one must read his *On the Kabbalah and Its Symbolism*. Another book, *The Messianic Idea*, also contains some very important essays on Lurianic Kabbalah, the "Jewish" star, etc. Scholem's essays in the new *Encyclopaedia Judaica* have been collected into *Kabbalah*, and here, too, one can get a very broad view of the field by the outstanding scholar in it. The serious student is urged to study these essays carefully.

In the area of general Jewish mysticism, one should read A. J. Heschel, "The Mystical Element in Judaism," in *The Jews,* ed. L. Finkelstein; reprinted in *Understanding Rabbinic Judaism,* ed. J. Neusner. "Jewish Mysticism" by G. Vajda, in the new edition of the *Encyclopaedia Britannica,* is certainly an important article. For scholars, the kaleidoscopic reviews of the field by G. Vajda in the *Revue de l'histoire des religions* (1955, 1963–64, and 1977) are indispensable.

There is a very beautifully written article by S. Schechter entitled "Safed in the Sixteenth Century," in his *Studies in Judaism, Second Series* (Philadelphia: Jewish Publication Society, 1908), dealing with the milieu of Luria. Also, Z. Werblowsky has written a very stimulating book on the same period entitled *Joseph Karo: Lawyer and Mystic*. In the area of the Merkabah literature, there is the scholarly essay of M. Smith, "Observations on *Heikhalot Rabbati,*" in *Biblical and Other Studies,* ed. A. Altmann. Lastly, there is J. Trachtenberg, *Jewish Magic and Superstition,* for the continuation of the magical tradition into the Middle Ages.

One fun project, which I have used as a final-examination topic, is to ask students to pick any one of the three dozen or so popular books on Jewish mysticism and write a critical book review. As one student remarked, "By the time I reached chapter four, I was alternately laughing and moaning."

THEMATIC INDEX*

---

*This is an index of themes and not only of words.